cooking
with the
sassy
mama

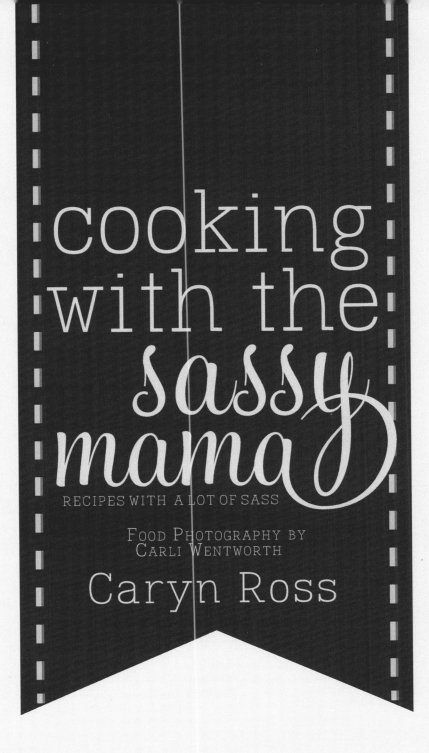

cooking with the sassy mama

RECIPES WITH A LOT OF SASS

FOOD PHOTOGRAPHY BY
CARLI WENTWORTH

Caryn Ross

TATE PUBLISHING
AND ENTERPRISES, LLC

Published by Tate Publishing & Enterprises, LLC
127 E. Trade Center Terrace | Mustang, Oklahoma 73064 USA
1.888.361.9473 | www.tatepublishing.com

Tate Publishing is committed to excellence in the publishing industry. The company reflects the philosophy established by the founders, based on Psalm 68:11,
"The Lord gave the word and great was the company of those who published it."

Book design copyright © 2012 by Tate Publishing, LLC. All rights reserved.
Cover design by Kenna Davis
Interior design by Joel Uber
Food photo credit to Carli Wentworth

Published in the United States of America

ISBN: 978-1-61346-728-2
1. Cooking; Regional & Ethnic, American, Middle Western States
2. Cooking; Courses & Dishes, General
12.11.26

Dedication

I lovingly dedicate this cookbook to my husband, Jack. His unconditional support and love is what inspired my goals and made them more than just a dream. I wake up every morning thanking my lucky stars that he picked me! He makes me feel every day that I am beautiful and capable of doing anything I set my mind to. For that alone I am blessed beyond measure. I love you with all of my heart.

To my children, Jackson and Caytie, this cookbook is a testament to dreaming big and pushing myself to break out of my comfort zone. Thank you for being my number one taste-testers!

To the women who have shaped the woman I am today: Mom, I miss you every day. I know that you are watching me from heaven, never doubting for a second I would end up here. You were always my cheerleader and encourager; almost always amused by my antics and other times fearful I might not find my way. But you allowed me to be creative and inspired me to "give it a whirl." Thank you, Mom. It worked! I am twirling and loving it!

Grandma, without your guidance and patience, I would never have learned to bake. Your concise explanations of baking left me hungry and curious for more.

Barbara, thank you for raising a son to cherish and respect his wife. Your drive and success have been a true inspiration to me. You are the bravest woman I have ever known. Anytime I feel like "maybe I can't," I think of you and pull on my XL big girl panties and get to to doin'!

Aunt Richadene, you taught me not to take myself too seriously. You show me all the time that family loves you in good times and bad times. I am forever blessed that you have loved me like your own! Best of all, thank you for teaching me to never take a bathtub for face value. After all, sometimes it's a slide!

Sunday, you were my arch nemesis as a kid. But now you are the best sister a girl could have. Your grace in the face of adversity is what gives me the energy to press forward. I aspire to have the dignity you possess on a daily basis. I love you.

Thank you to Linda Gibson, Barbara Ross, Mia Blake, and Gina Mitchell for being my sweet editors. This Mama can cook, but sometimes she needs help with crossing her T's and dotting her I's!

A huge thanks to Tim Higdon Photography for the beautiful cover shot! Thank you for making me look beautiful!

I also must thank The Nees Family for the use of their rocking awesome retro kitchen.

Table of Contents

Cake Dots

Simple Tips on How to Make a Happy Plate

I have to give it up to my children's preschool for inspiring my "Happy Plate" philosophy. At Pumpkin Shell Preschool in Norman, Oklahoma, the children are praised for eating all of their veggies by calling it a "happy plate." Jack and Caytie would come home each day to report that they had both a great day and a "happy plate." The concept stuck with me, and I found myself using the same term at home with our family meals.

During the early years of motherhood, I often felt in a fog just trying to find my brain in the midst of laundry, *Barney* videos, and play dates. One thing I found that brought me a semblance of creativity was cooking. It was my go-to activity when I was feeling happy, stressed, sad, or even when I just needed a little order (after all, cooking requires you to measure, stir, and pour all in a certain order). As we all know, motherhood has no order. It's all about controlled chaos. So when I was in a tizzy, I looked no further than my kitchen to bring me some peace.

You might be wondering how in the world this mama made it in the cooking world. The answer is really quite simple. I had to stop sittin' on my biscuit, never going to risk it, and finally go for it! During those early motherly years, I was forever sitting on the couch watching cooking shows for a few stolen minutes. Not only was I inspired to get in the kitchen; I began feeling like I would love to show people *my* tips, *my* tricks, and *my* delicious recipes. But how? There are no producers or cooking talent agents roaming around in Oklahoma. So in 2010 I entered my first and only cooking contest sponsored by Philadelphia Cream Cheese and Paula Deen. All I had to do was send in videos of me cooking, submit my recipe, and hope that someone in Hollywood would take notice! As luck and lots of hard work would have it, they picked me to be a finalist. After a screen test and filming with Paula Deen, I was picked as the Appetizer Host of Real Women of Philadelphia in June 2010. Since then, I have made it my mission to show families how to prepare meals with sass, hoping that will bring them back to the table! After all, that is where all good things happen.

If I could offer one bit of advice on how to make a meal with sass, it would be to think of it as an extension of you and of your love for others. Food is what we bring when we celebrate birthdays or the birth of a baby, and it is also one of the first items to appear when someone is mourning the loss of a loved one. In our society, food equals love.

My book will show you how to make simple, delicious food that anyone would be proud to present. I also will share some of my secrets tips and tricks to guarantee you knock their socks off! This mama will even tell you that cooking is not always perfect or beautiful. In the end, if it tastes great and you didn't have to call the fire department, then consider that a success.

My number one tip with cooking is to cook with a purpose. Sounds like a no-brainer, but many times cooking can be drudgery if you let it. I try to create meals for someone special. So, for example, if we are watching TV or looking at magazines and the kids say, "That looks good," then I make a mental note of that and try to prepare a meal inspired by what they liked. You will find that your family and friends are perfect muses for your cooking. After all, we love them, and food is love too!

My philosophy that food is love is really quite simple. It is one of our basic needs, similar to oxygen. Think about it. When we are born, the first thing someone does is feed us. Food is comfort. So I got to thinking that when I cook, I'm showing love to others. Now don't get me wrong. I'm not always June Cleaver. I don't skip to the table holding a bowl filled with mashed potatoes. But I do prepare those mashed potatoes with my love, my effort, and my energy. So why not make those the best darn mashed potatoes on the planet?

There is one bit of wisdom that my mom force-fed me as a child: "Do not go to anyone's home without *something* in your hands to share." To this day, whenever I step into a person's home, I am faithful to never come empty-handed. I know my mother would be proud knowing I have shared her advice and taught it to my own children. A little hospitality and thinking of others is always a sure-fire way to make your presence memorable.

Also, keep an eye out for my "Kitchen Nuggets" throughout the book. Let's just say that anyone who has been cooking as long as I have has endured their share of total disasters! My "Kitchen Nuggets" are special hints here and there to help make the dish the best it can be and save you from making a mess of your own.

Appetizers

When I was growing up, I never had an appetizer in a restaurant. One of the greatest thrills of "growing up" was realizing if I wanted an appetizer, I could order it for myself. My husband and I are famous for ordering two or three appetizers before dinner. I love the allure of huge flavor in a small bite, and I've seen some truly artistic presentations that make this small meal "before the big one" a real treat.

However, there is nothing worse than trying to over think an appetizer before the meal. One of my all-time greatest recipes came from desperation at sea. We were in our boat headed from Key West to Fort Meyers when the engines shut down and we were stranded in the middle of the Gulf. So while my husband called Sea Tow to tow us back to shore, I did what any good captain's wife would do: alert the crew to eat the perishables! We proceeded to mow through the ice cream sandwiches and yogurt quickly. However, we needed something more munchable. So I opened up the fridge, took out the cream cheese, bacon, green onions, and mayo, and proceeded to invent my "Bigger Than Your Butt Dip," simply named out of the fear that eating all this was going to result in more "junk in my trunk" once we hit land. For over eight hours we bobbed in the ocean, talked to the curious dolphins around us, and ate my "Bigger Than Your Butt Dip." It was simple, delicious, and just the thing to pass the time and fill our bellies.

The biggest lesson is *don't* stress over it. Just get in there and make something memorable, and I promise your appetizer will be off and flying—or in our case, floating!

Garlic Beer Cheese Dip

1 8-oz. pkg. cream cheese, softened

1 tsp. garlic, minced

2 c. shredded sharp cheddar cheese

8 oz. Velveeta, cubed

1/2 lb. thick cut bacon, cooked crisp and crumbled. (In a pinch I use
   Hormel Real Bacon Bits)

1/2 c. beer

1/4 tsp. red pepper flakes

2 green onions, chopped

In a large saucepan, add softened cream cheese, garlic, sharp cheese, and Velveeta. Heat on medium heat until melted and well combined. Stir often. Pour in beer. Once the cheese and beer are well combined, pour into a slow cooker set on "low." Top with bacon and green onions. Stir frequently to combine and melt.

Serve with pretzel chips or corn chips!

Serves: 8-10 people

Kitchen Nugget: I always spray my slow cooker with a nonstick cooking spray to help prevent the cheese sauce from sticking!

This Ain't No Hidden Valley Ranch Dip Mix

This was my mom's recipe, and it is still the best recipe I know of to make ranch dressing and dip. Gone are the days of that mystery powder you buy in the pouch. These are the real herbs and spices mixed with buttermilk and mayonnaise. I make this mix in large batches to give as gifts!

    8 tsp. dried minced onion
    1 T. dried parsley flakes
    1 tsp. paprika
    2 tsp. sugar
    2 tsp. salt
    2 tsp. pepper
    1 1/2 tsp. garlic powder

Additional ingredients for dressing:
    1 c. mayonnaise
    1 c. buttermilk

Additional ingredients for dip:
    1 c. sour cream

In a small bowl, combine the first seven ingredients. Store in an airtight container in a cool, dry place for up to one year. I store mine in a mason jar.

To prepare dressing: In a bowl, combine 1 tablespoon of mix with mayonnaise and buttermilk. Stir well and refrigerate for at least three hours before serving.

To prepare dip: In a bowl, combine 1 tablespoon mix and sour cream. Stir well and refrigerate for at least 1 hour before serving.

 Kitchen Nugget: Mason jars are my favorite way to store my dried herb mixes as well as any salad dressings in the refrigerator. To serve, just give your jar a shake, and your dressing will be perfectly mixed and ready to enjoy.

Buffalo Chicken Sliders

This is the perfect "man food" for game days or when you just have a bunch of guys around. Everyone loves buffalo chicken, so why not stick it on a bun, dress it up a bit, and have a whole lot of *yum*?

12 chicken tenders, grilled
1 8-oz. pkg. cream cheese, softened
1 c. bleu cheese, crumbled
1/4 tsp. red pepper flakes
1/2 bottle of Frank's Wing Sauce
1/4 c. melted butter
1 pkg. of King Hawaiian butter rolls

In a small bowl, combine cream cheese, bleu cheese crumbles, and 1/4 teaspoon of red pepper. Set aside.

Grill chicken tenders till done, and set aside to cool. In a large bowl, mix together the wing sauce and melted butter. Now add chicken and toss to coat in sauce. Set aside to till ready to assemble sliders.

Cut Hawaiian rolls in half, place a chicken tender on one side, and spread bleu cheese cream mixture on other half. Put together and serve with celery sticks.

Kitchen Nugget: Use any leftover cheese mixture as a dip for celery!

Herb Cheese Spread

My favorite appetizer has always been cheese and crackers. Nothing makes me happier than a variety of cheeses, summer sausage, and some sort of herbed cheese spread arranged on a tray. This is one of my favorites, and it is a staple onboard our boat, the *Sassy*. Tastes eerily similar to a brand name cheese spread…

  2 8-oz. pkg. cream cheese, softened
  4 oz. butter (softened)
  1 tsp. oregano
  1/4 tsp. dill
  1/4 tsp. basil
  1/4 tsp. thyme
  1/4 tsp. marjoram
  1/4 tsp. freshly ground pepper
  2 cloves garlic, chopped

Prepare four ramekin containers by lining the inside with clear plastic wrap. Allow about 2 inches of overhang on the top. Place all ingredients into a food processor and pulse till combined. Remove from food processor and store in an airtight container. Press cheese mixture into ramekins till it reaches the top. Smooth top with offset spatula. Cover with the leftover plastic wrap. Refrigerate at least 4 hours before serving. To serve, remove cheese from ramekin, unwrap, and place on a platter. Super with pita chips or water crackers.

Bigger Than Your Butt Dip

I make this dip in mass quantities during football season. I take it to all the tailgate parties, and now I can't show up without it or I'd have some really unhappy friends! It is perfect on your favorite cracker or chip.

2 8-oz. pkg. cream cheese, softened
2 c. crisply cooked hickory smoked thick cut bacon, crumbled
1 c. mayonnaise
5 chopped green onions
2 c. grated sharp cheddar cheese
1 tsp. seasoning salt
1/2 tsp. pepper

In a large bowl, mix all ingredients together. Once mixed well, place in an airtight container. Chill at least 4 hours before serving.

Kitchen Nugget: This dip is perfect placed by heaping spoonfuls in baked potatoes.

Piggy Puffs

This is the creation I made to fancy up my Bigger Than Your Butt Dip. I have to say it is pretty tasty. However, I do have to warn you: get ready to be asked for this recipe all the time! I send this recipe to someone at least once a week. Don't say I didn't warn you!

>1 8-oz. pkg. Philadelphia cream cheese
>1 pkg. puff pastry sheets, thawed
>1 3-oz. pkg. Oscar Meyer real bacon bits and pieces
>1/2 c. mayonnaise
>2 c. Kraft shredded sharp cheddar cheese
>1/2 c. Parmesan cheese, grated
>4 green onions, chopped

Preheat oven to 400 degrees. Allow puff pastry to thaw on counter per package instructions. Mix together the cream cheese and mayonnaise till smooth. Add in bacon, green onions, Parmesan cheese, and sharp cheese. Stir until well combined.

Once puff pastry is thawed, unfold 1 sheet. Cut the sheet into thirds vertically. (I follow the lines from the folds.) Then cut each third in 1/2 vertically. Then cut the dough in 1/2 horizontally. Cut the horizontal pieces in 1/2 again (essentially fourths). That should make 24 pieces total.

In a well-greased mini-muffin tin, press a square into each hole. Stretch the square a bit so the pastry covers the sides. Place 1-2 teaspoons of bacon cream cheese mixture on top of pastry and press into dough.

Bake puffs for 12-15 minutes or until golden brown. Allow puffs to cool slightly before removing from tin. Place on platter and serve warm!

Serves: 48 puffs

Mango Shrimp Salad Cups

Are you in a pinch to make something delicious yet pretty? Well these little phyllo shrimp salad cups are the perfect thing. Delicate cups filled with a mango-infused creamy shrimp salad. They are sure to impress and take you away to the tropics in one bite!

1 lb. frozen small cooked shrimp, thawed

1/2 c. chopped mango

4 T. shredded coconut, toasted

1/4 c. pineapple tidbits drained, but reserve juice

2 green onions, chopped

1/2 c. mayonnaise

2 tsp. honey

1/2 tsp. curry powder

1 tsp. pineapple juice

2 pkg. phyllo cups (15 count), thawed

Thaw phyllo cups on countertop. Allow shrimp to thaw under cool water. Rinse and dry thoroughly. Place in large mixing bowl.

Chop mango into a small dice and add to mixing bowl. Add the toasted coconut, green onions, and pineapple tidbits.

In small bowl, combine mayonnaise, curry powder, honey, and pineapple juice. Stir till well blended.

Fold creamy mixture into large mixing bowl. Combine the two mixtures completely. Spoon shrimp salad mixture into phyllo cups. Garnish with toasted coconut.

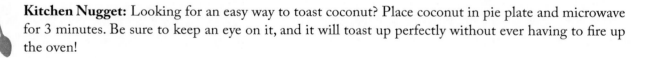

Kitchen Nugget: Looking for an easy way to toast coconut? Place coconut in pie plate and microwave for 3 minutes. Be sure to keep an eye on it, and it will toast up perfectly without ever having to fire up the oven!

Easy Chai Tea Mix

During the fall and winter, this is what I keep stocked to drink each night before bed. The warm milky tea with the comforting spices of cinnamon and nutmeg lull me to sleep. I love to give this to friends during the holidays, and now it has become a staple in many pantries around town! You can easily substitute the sugar with a sweetener to lighten it up a bit.

1 c. nonfat dry milk powder
1 c. nondairy powdered coffee creamer
1 c. French vanilla-flavored nondairy powdered coffee creamer
2 1/2 c. sugar
1 1/2 c. unsweetened instant tea
2 tsp. ground ginger
2 tsp. cinnamon
1 tsp. ground cardamom
1 tsp. nutmeg
1 tsp. allspice
1 tsp. white pepper

Add all of the above ingredients into a large bowl. Mix well. Once the mixture is combined place in an airtight container to store.

To make tea, add 2 tablespoons of chai tea mix to an 8-ounce glass of hot water. Stir and enjoy!

Hot Buttered Chai: add 1/2 cup of chai tea mix to 1 pint of vanilla bean ice cream. Mix together and return to freezer. Simply add one scoop to a mug, pour hot water over, stir, and drink! (You can even add a jigger of rum for some extra toastiness.)

Summertime Bourbon Slush

Nothing tastes better on a hot summer day than a slushy cocktail. This recipe is super simple and freezes well in a bucket in the freezer. My mom served this all the time, and thankfully I was able to find the recipe to share with you.

4 small Lipton tea bags
9 c. water
2 1/4 c. Bourbon
1/4 c. Triple Sec
3 cans frozen lemonade, thawed

Boil 2 cups of water, and then add the tea bags. Allow to steep and then cool. In large plastic container add tea, Bourbon, Triple Sec, lemonade, and remaining water. Stir and combine well. Place in freezer for 24 hours.

To serve slush: Scrape with spoon and place in high ball glass. Top with 7-Up or Sprite.

Soups and Salads

I grew up dreading salad. In our house, iceberg lettuce with a slice of cucumber and a tomato wedge was the only salad I knew. Once I left home and started to travel, I was introduced to the world of greens, roots, nuts, cheeses, and veggies. It was refreshing to learn that the "lettuce" portion of the salad is many times just the base. All of the true flavor of the salad comes from the various toppings, amazing dressings, and vinaigrettes!

My piece of advice when it comes to salads: put that fork of bland down and go find something green! When I travel, there is nothing better than visiting a local farmer's market. My family and I have tasted fresh fruit and veggies from San Francisco to New Jersey. You would be amazed at the different items each city presented depending on the time of year. In January, California was bursting with strawberries that my husband would buy by the case. I would then lose sight of him, only to find him resting on a curb, munching away happily in strawberry bliss. Nothing makes me happier than eating and shopping, and farmer's markets offer the best of both!

Soups for my family range from old-fashioned chicken noodle to crab bisque. The one thing we can all agree on is that the soup *must be hot!* Nothing makes us crazier than cold soup.

The only deviation from that rule is when I order fresh gazpacho in Florida. And every time, like clockwork, I hear the same commentary from Jack and kids: "Why in the world do they call that soup? It should be called salsa…or how about, blended-up garden leftovers!" No matter what they say, I just smile and eat my summer goodness in a bowl.

In any case, I love it, and eventually when the weather turns hot enough, they start asking for a bowl! If they're lucky, I might even let them use a chip to dip in…

Whatever the case may be with your family, I encourage you to give options when creating soup. Perhaps one child likes mushrooms and the other doesn't. There is no rule that says you can't serve various vegetables in small bowls on the table and call it Potluck Soup Night! Each person simply adds their favorite veggies and toppings to the soup base. Trust me. There is nothing kids enjoy more than having options!

Bibb Salad with Zippy Ranch

Here in the Midwest you cannot find a single restaurant that does not serve ranch dressing. I love the delicate crispness of Bibb lettuce with a creamy yet spicy ranch dressing. This salad is perfectly paired with grilled steak and baked potatoes.

1 clove garlic, peeled and chopped (about 1/2 tsp.)
1 c. buttermilk
1/3 c. mayonnaise
1/3 c. sour cream
2 T. fresh flat-leaf parsley, chopped
2 T. fresh chives, chopped
1 green onion, thinly sliced (about 2 T.)
1 tsp. white wine vinegar
1 tsp. smoked paprika
4 heads (Boston or Bibb) lettuce, torn
1 c. yellow or red pear tomatoes, halved
1/2 cucumber, sliced thin

For Zippy Ranch Dressing: In a medium-sized bowl, place garlic in the bowl. Whisk buttermilk, mayonnaise, sour cream, parsley, chives, green onion, vinegar, paprika, and 1/4 teaspoon black pepper into garlic until combined.

In a large salad bowl, toss lettuce with tomatoes and sliced cucumbers.

Serve with Zippy Ranch dressing.

Serves: 8

Caprese Picnic Salad with Easy Balsamic Vinaigrette

Picnics in the spring and summer are a favorite of mine. The usual hamburgers and hot dogs can get pretty boring, which is why I love to serve a super salad! I make this salad ahead of time and store it in airtight plastic containers. This ensures easy transport and helps the salad remain cold in your cooler.

> 3 c. grape tomatoes, cut in half
>
> 2 c. of fresh mozzarella, cut into bite-size pieces
>
> 1/4 c. fresh basil, chopped
>
> 1/2 tsp. kosher salt
>
> 1/2 tsp. fresh grated pepper
>
> 1/4 cup sliced sun-dried tomatoes in oil, julienned

In a large bowl, mix together the tomatoes, mozzarella, and basil. Toss with dressing and place in an airtight container. Refrigerate at least 4 hours before serving.

Dressing:

> 1/4 c. balsamic vinegar
>
> 2 tsp. dark brown sugar
>
> 2 cloves garlic, chopped
>
> 1/2 tsp. salt
>
> 1/2 tsp. freshly ground black pepper
>
> 1/4 tsp. red pepper (more if you like spicy)
>
> 3/4 c. olive oil

In a small bowl, add the balsamic vinegar and brown sugar. Whisk together till well combined. Add garlic, red pepper, salt, and pepper and stir. While whisking liquid, pour the olive oil in slowly, whisking well until the oil is completely emulsified.

Kitchen Nugget: Sometimes I serve this over mixed greens with quiche or a chicken salad. It makes a perfect luncheon salad.

Cranberry Spinach Salad with Toasty Brie Bites

In the wintertime, I find this to be the perfect salad. Cranberries, spinach, and pumpkins are always easy to find. A perfect salad to make for the holidays. Festive with green and red!

2/3 c. fresh or frozen cranberries

1/4 c. sugar

1/4 c. white wine vinegar

1/4 c. orange juice

2 tsp. Dijon-style mustard

3/4 c. olive oil

2 tsp. finely snipped fresh sage

1/2 tsp. kosher salt or salt

1/4 tsp. freshly ground black pepper

16 1/4-inch slices baguette, toasted

8 oz. Brie cheese, cut in 16 wedges

10 c. baby spinach

1/2 c. dried cranberries

1/4 c. shelled pumpkin seeds, toasted (optional)

For the dressing: in a saucepan, combine cranberries, sugar, and vinegar. Cook over medium heat, stirring often, 5 minutes or until cranberries soften and begin to pop. Remove from heat; cool.

Transfer cranberry mixture to blender. Blend on high until nearly smooth. Add orange juice and mustard; process to blend. With blender running, slowly pour in oil until slightly thickened and creamy. Transfer to bowl. Whisk in sage, salt, and pepper.

For Brie toast: preheat the broiler. Place wedge of cheese on each toasted bread slice. Broil 5 or so inches from heat till toasty.

To serve: toss spinach, dried cranberries, and seeds with 3/4 cup of the dressing. Serve with brie toast. Pass additional dressing.

Serves: 8

Steakhouse Chopped Salad

After eating at a certain well-known steakhouse. I left craving their chopped salad. So I went to task, remembering all of the ingredients, and recreated my own version. I have to say it is pretty darn close to the original. I especially love the creamy lemon basil dressing (see page 45).

1 head of iceberg lettuce, chopped

3 c. baby spinach, chopped

1/2 c. red onion, finely chopped

1/2 c. fresh mushrooms, chopped fine

1/4 c. green olives, chopped fine

8 slices thick-cut hickory smoked bacon, cooked crisp and chopped fine

2 eggs hardboiled, chopped fine

1/4 c. hearts of palm, chopped fine

1 c. herb seasoned croutons

1/2 c. bleu cheese, crumbled

1 c. cherry tomatoes, halved

1 c. crispy fried onions; I use French's

Chop the lettuce and spinach and place in a large salad bowl.

Then chop all of the above ingredients and place on top of the lettuce mixture.

To serve the salad, I toss all of the ingredients with enough dressing to coat. Then I use a clean can that has had both ends removed. Place can on a plate and add in salad 2/3 of the way filled. Gently remove can and top with fried onions and bleu cheese crumbles. Voila! Fancy salad that doesn't taste fancy!

Serves: 4 servings

Lemon Basil Dressing

1 c. mayonnaise
Freshly squeezed juice of 1 lemon
1/2 c. fresh basil leaves, very thinly sliced
Coarse salt, to taste
Freshly ground pepper, to taste

Combine all ingredients in a small jar, cover, and shake well. For a creamier texture, mix in a blender. Place in refrigerator and allow to sit at least 4 hours before serving. Pour the dressing over the top of salad and toss.

Tearoom Blueberry Salad

Ladies love a tearoom for the pastries, salads, and tea. This blueberry gelatin salad pairs beautifully with a green salad or a chilled chicken salad. I like to think of it as a dessert salad.

2 (3 oz.) pkg. of grape Jell-O

2 c. boiling water

1 (8 oz.) can crushed pineapple, drained

1 can size blueberry pie filling

1 (8 oz.) pkg. cream cheese

1 c. sour cream

1/2 c. sugar

1 tsp. vanilla

1/2 c. chopped pecans

Drain pineapple; reserve juice. Dissolve Jell-O in boiling water; stir in reserved pineapple juice. Chill until slightly set, about the consistency of an unbeaten egg white. Stir in pineapple and blueberry pie filling. Pour into a 9 1/2-x-6-x-2-inch pan; chill until firm. Combine sour cream, cream cheese, and sugar; mix well until smooth and well blended. Spread over blueberry Jell-O salad and top with chopped pecans or walnuts. Cut into squares and serve.

Serves: 12

Mermaid Soup

When it's cold outside, nothing sounds better than a big, hearty bowl of soup. I started making this when my kids were little, and they named it Mermaid Soup because of the little shell-shaped pasta. This soup is perfect for kids because it is packed with vegetables in a hearty sauce.

2 T. extra-virgin olive oil
4 slices uncooked thick-sliced hickory smoked bacon, chopped
2 sprigs rosemary, left whole
1 tsp. fresh thyme, chopped
1 dried Bay leaf
1 large onion, finely chopped
3 carrots, finely chopped
2 ribs celery, finely chopped
4 large cloves garlic, chopped
Salt and pepper
2 (15 oz.) cans cannellini beans
2 can size fire-roasted tomatoes
2 c. water
1 qt. chicken stock, low salt
1 1/2 c. small pasta shells
Grated Parmigiano-Reggiano

Heat a large stockpot over medium heat and add oil and bacon. Brown bacon and add herbs, stems and all, bay leaf, carrot, onion, celery, garlic, salt and pepper to taste. Add beans, fire-roasted tomatoes, water, and stock. Heat on high until soup begins to boil. Add in small pasta shells. Reduce heat to medium and cook until shells are al dente. Remove the bay leaves. To serve, spoon into bowls and top with Parmigiano-Reggiano cheese. Serve with a crusty baguette and olive oil for dipping.

Serves: 6

Kitchen Nugget: Make a double batch and place the leftovers in jars to give as gifts! Just add a tag, and it will keep for a week in the refrigerator!

Weeknight Potato Soup

This is my friend Kerrie's recipe that she makes every Halloween. It is my favorite potato soup, and once she shared the recipe with me, I was stunned to learn the potatoes are actually packaged frozen hash browns!

1 pkg. frozen hash browns, cubed type, thawed
1 stick unsalted butter
2 ribs celery, chopped
1 small onion, chopped
1 can size cream of chicken soup
1 pint half-n-half
2 c. whole milk
1 c. shredded cheddar cheese

Toppings:

Sharp cheese
Green onions, chopped
Thick sliced bacon, cooked crisp and crumbled
Fried onions

In a stockpot, sauté onions and celery in butter over medium heat. Cook till onions are translucent and celery is tender. Add hash browns, cream of chicken soup, half-and-half, whole milk, and cheese. Heat gently until warm. Serve and garnish with suggested toppings.

Serves: 6

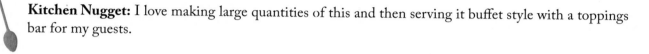

Kitchen Nugget: I love making large quantities of this and then serving it buffet style with a toppings bar for my guests.

Broccoli and Leek Cheddar Soup

This recipe came about when I was trying to use up a leek. I was at a loss as to what to do with a single leek, so I cut it up and added it to my broccoli and cheese soup. This soup is perfectly creamy with a hint of onion and cheddar.

> 1 stick unsalted butter
> 1 medium onion, chopped
> 2 leeks, chopped white portion
> 2 garlic cloves, minced
> 3 c. low-sodium chicken broth
> 1 (16-oz.) pkg. broccoli florets, thawed
> 2 1/2 c. 2-percent, reduced-fat milk
> 1/3 c. cornstarch
> 1/4 tsp. black pepper
> 1 c. sharp cheese, shredded
> 8 oz. processed cheese, cubed (such as Velveeta)

Heat a large stockpot over medium-high heat. First melt butter. Add onion, leeks, and garlic; sauté 3 minutes or until tender. Add broth and broccoli. Bring broccoli mixture to a boil over medium-high heat. Reduce heat to medium; cook 10 minutes.

Combine milk and cornstarch, stirring with a whisk until well blended. Add milk mixture to broccoli mixture. Cook 5 minutes or until slightly thick, stirring constantly. Stir in pepper. Remove from heat; add sharp cheese and Velveeta, stirring until cheese melts.

Using an immersion blender, pulse until soup is smooth. Serve and top with parsley.

Serves: 6

Fire-Roasted Tomato Basil Soup

This soup feeds the soul and makes you feel like you're sitting in your favorite lunch spot. I always have the makings for this recipe in my pantry ready to go. I've even made a double batch and frozen half in resealable plastic bags. I then deliver them as gifts to sick friends in need of some warm comfort in a bowl.

1 onion, chopped
2 cloves garlic, chopped fine
Olive oil
4 can size of fire roasted tomatoes
1 large can size crushed tomatoes
1 T. dried basil
1/2 tsp. thyme
2 T. brown sugar
1 tsp. pepper
Salt to taste
2 c. half-and-half
Parmesan cheese
Fresh basil

In a 2-quart stockpot over medium heat, cook onion and garlic in olive oil until onion is soft. Be careful not to burn the garlic! Add in the fire-roasted tomatoes, crushed tomatoes, basil, thyme, salt, pepper, and brown sugar.

Using a blender or immersion blender, puree soup until smooth; return to pan if using blender. Whisk in half-and-half. Heat through, being very careful not to boil the soup. Boiling will cause milk to separate and make for a lumpy soup.

Serve warm and garnish with freshly grated Parmesan and fresh basil.

Serves: 6

Foxy White Chicken Chili

This hearty white chili is my favorite recipe made by my best girlfriend, Gina. She serves it at football watch parties and then has a topping bar to add to the yumminess! Perfect to make in large quantities for a big, hungry crowd.

> 1 (12 oz.) jar salsa verde
> 3 c. cooked rotisserie chicken, shredded
> 1 (15 oz.) can cannellini beans, drained
> 4 c. chicken broth
> 1 tsp. ground cumin
> Mexican Crema*
> Shredded Mexican blend cheese
> Fritos corn chips

Empty the salsa into a large saucepan. Cook 2 minutes over medium high heat; then add the chicken, beans, broth, and cumin. Bring to a boil, lower heat to a simmer, and cook for 10 minutes; stirring occasionally. Top each bowl with a handful of Fritos, a dollop of Mexican Crema*, and cheese.

Serves: 4

*Mexican Crema is a cross between crème fraîche and sour cream. It is a lighter, creamier alternative that does not break down as much in hot liquids. Perfect for soups and chilis.

Brunch and Breads

Baking is my therapy. I love nothing more after an extra-stressful day than to tie on my apron and get to measuring. When I bake, there is order, and the outcome is always pleasing.

I first began baking when I was nine years old. My grandma taught me to make her legendary "rolls" by allowing me to have my own bowl. When she measured, I measured. When she stirred, I stirred. She sat patiently by as I spilled flour on the floor, dropped the egg shell in the mixture, and nearly upended the whole bowl trying to stir everything together just right. She did all of this while gently encouraging me.

Grandma also explained to me the "whys" of baking—how yeast needs sugar, why level measuring is crucial to insure a perfectly risen cake, and how to properly cream sugar and butter. She told me those two ingredients were the base of all the goodness in our cookies and cakes. I could have learned all of these tips, tricks, and methods from a cookbook, but nothing beats hands-on education. Thankfully I was blessed to have my grandma as my mentor.

However, I need you to know that I am in no way perfect in the kitchen. In fact, some of my best kitchen defeats have occurred while baking. One year I got up at the crack of dawn to make those elusive rolls of Grandma's, only to grab the wrong container, which held wheat germ instead of yeast. Only after hours of talking and praying over that depressing bread did my mom realize what I had done. She brought out the offending container and announced that this stuff would never rise and I better get to cracking open some Hungry Jack biscuits!

Needless to say that year instead of feasting upon warm, buttery crescent rolls, we had dense buttery hockey pucks for Thanksgiving. I have yet to live down that baking slip-up.

Unfortunately my biggest disaster was yet to be! It happened later that year when I was baking a treat for a friend in Estes Park, Colorado. What should have been a decadent bar, my dessert, was dubbed the greatest bird feeder treats my friend had ever seen! I take comfort knowing even that wasn't a complete failure. Just ask the birds!

So today I always plan ahead a little bit. Baking should be a snap, and a brunch will be up and going in no time. Remember, good preparation is the key. (Not to mention well-labeled containers!)

Breakfast Apricot Scones

When I was a kid, my mom would make these buttery scones, and we always counted down the minutes until they were ready. There is still almost nothing better on a cold winter morning than a warm scone and a cup of tea.

4 1/4 c. all purpose flour
1/4 c. sugar, plus turbinado sugar, for sprinkling
2 T. baking powder
2 tsp. kosher salt
1 T. grated lemon zest
3 sticks cold unsalted butter, chopped into small bits
2 T. sour cream
4 large eggs, lightly beaten
1 tsp. vanilla paste
3/4 c. heavy whipping cream
1 c. dried apricots, chopped into bite-sized pieces
1 egg
2 T. whipping cream

Glaze

2/3 c. powdered sugar
4 tsp. apricot nectar
1/2 tsp. vanilla paste

Preheat the oven to 400 degrees.

In the bowl of an electric mixer, mix 4 cups of flour, 1/4 cup sugar, baking powder, salt, and lemon zest. Add the cold butter, and mix at the lowest speed until the butter is the size of small crumbles. Combine the eggs, vanilla paste, sour cream, and heavy cream. With the mixer on low speed, slowly pour into the flour and butter mixture. Mix until just blended. The dough will look lumpy! Do not overmix; just allow it to come together.

Combine the dried apricots with an additional 1/4 cup of flour, add to the dough, and mix on low speed until just combined.

Dump the dough onto a floured mat or countertop. Knead dough into a ball, adding additional flour as needed to keep from sticking to your hands. It will not be smooth like a bread dough, so don't overwork. Makes for a tough scone. Shape the dough into a circle which is between 3/4 and 1 inch thick. Cut into wedges like a pizza or use a round cookie cutter for smaller scones.

After cutting, place the scones on a parchment-lined baking sheet at least 1 inch apart. Beat egg into whipping cream. Brush with whipping cream mixture and place in the hot oven. Bake for 30-40 minutes or until golden brown.

Allow the scones to cool for 15 minutes and then whisk together the confectioners' sugar and apricot nectar. Drizzle over the scones. Serve warm.

Serves: a dozen scones cut into triangles

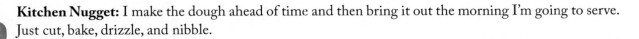

Kitchen Nugget: I make the dough ahead of time and then bring it out the morning I'm going to serve. Just cut, bake, drizzle, and nibble.

Peaches and Cream Coffee Cake

This cinnamon almond coffee cake is the perfect blend of cake and sweet nuttiness. It is the cake most requested by my girlfriends whenever we all get together for coffee talk.

1 1/2 sticks unsalted butter, softened
1 1/2 c. sugar
3 large eggs, at room temperature
1 1/2 tsp. vanilla paste
1 tsp. almond extract
1 1/4 c. sour cream
2 1/2 c. cake flour
2 tsp. baking powder
1/2 tsp. baking soda
1/2 tsp. kosher salt

Cinnamon Crumble Filling

1/4 c. brown sugar, packed
1/2 c. all-purpose flour
1 1/2 tsp. ground cinnamon
1/4 tsp. kosher salt
3 T. cold unsalted butter, cut into pieces
3/4 c. chopped almonds

Peaches and Cream Filling

1/2 c. peach preserves
1/4 c. sugar
8 oz. container cream cheese, tub container

Glaze

1/2 c. confectioners' sugar
1 tsp. vanilla paste
1/2 tsp. peach schnapps
2 T. whipping cream

Preheat the oven to 350 degrees. Grease and flour a 10-inch tube pan.

In the bowl of an electric mixer, cream together the butter and sugar until light (at least 3 minutes). Add eggs one at a time; then add in almond extract, vanilla paste, and sour cream. In a medium-sized bowl combine the dry ingredients: flour, baking powder, baking soda, and salt. Slowly add flour mixture to wet ingredients, being careful to only mix till well combined.

To assemble the cinnamon crumble streusel mixture, simply combine all the dry ingredients in a medium-sized bowl. Add in cold butter and, using your fingers or a pastry blender, incorporate butter bits with dry ingredients till crumbles form. Mix in the almonds.

To assemble the cream cheese filling, simply mix together the cream cheese and sugar till smooth.

Pour half of the cake batter into the bottom of the tube pan, spreading to cover entire bottom. Sprinkle with half of the streusel topping. Next, place dollops of peach preserves and the cream cheese mixture, making sure not to get too close to the edges. Add remaining batter and spread to completely seal edges. Top with remaining streusel topping. Tap cake on the counter to help remove any bubbles. Place into hot oven and bake for 50-60 minutes or until cake tester comes out clean.

While cake is baking, make the peach glaze. In a small bowl, combine the powdered sugar, vanilla paste, peach schnapps, and whipping cream. Stir till smooth. Set aside.

Allow cake to cool, and then remove from tube pan and place on plate. Drizzle peach glaze over the top of the cake. Serve!

Kitchen Nugget: This is a perfect cake to give as a gift for a new baby, as a housewarming gift, or to a sick friend.

Chocolate Zucchini Bread

This is a super-moist quick bread and an excellent way to use up your summer zucchini bounty. I remember my neighbor making this all summer long when I was a kid. It was my favorite chocolate bread, and then when I found out it was made from squash, I was totally floored.

- 2 c. flour, plus an additional 2 tsp.
- 2 tsp. cinnamon
- 1/2 tsp. salt
- 1 1/2 tsp. baking soda
- 6 T. unsweetened cocoa powder
- 1/2 c. canola oil
- 1 c. sugar
- 1/4 c. brown sugar
- 3 eggs
- 2 tsp. vanilla
- 1/2 c. sour cream
- 3 c. grated zucchini
- 3/4 c. mini chocolate chips

Preheat oven to 350 degrees. Butter and flour 2 loaf pans and set aside.

Mix topping ingredients in a small bowl and set aside.

Place flour, cinnamon, baking soda, salt, and cocoa powder in a small bowl and whisk to combine. Set aside.

Using a hand mixer, beat oil, white sugar, brown sugar, and eggs until combined and slightly fluffy, 1-2 minutes. Add vanilla and sour cream, and mix. Fold in the zucchini. One cup at a time, add in flour mixture, and mix. Add chocolate chips. Stir. Place equal amounts of batter into each loaf pan. Bake for one hour or until toothpick comes out clean. Cool and enjoy. Store in an airtight container.

Donut Muffins

This recipe came about when my family was snowed in and craving donuts. So I decided to try making muffins that taste like donuts, and that's how this little gem came about. Now it's a staple on our weekend breakfast table.

1/2 c. sugar
1/4 c. unsalted butter, melted
3/4 tsp. ground nutmeg
1/2 c. whole milk
1 tsp. baking powder
1 c. all purpose flour

Topping

1/4 c. unsalted butter, melted
1/2 c. sugar
1 tsp. ground cinnamon

Preheat oven to 375 degrees. Grease muffin tin well.

Mix 1/2 cup sugar, 1/4 cup melted butter, and nutmeg in a large bowl. Stir in the milk; then mix in the baking powder and flour until just combined. Fill the prepared muffin cups about half full.

Bake in the preheated oven until the tops are lightly golden, 15 to 20 minutes.

While muffins are baking, place 1/4 cup of melted butter in a bowl. In a separate bowl, mix together 1/2 cup of sugar with the cinnamon. Remove muffins from the tin, dip each muffin in the melted butter, and roll in the sugar-cinnamon mixture. Let cool and serve.

Serves: 12 muffins or 24 mini muffins

Tropical Granola

I started making this recipe when we were in spending our summer sailing around the Bahamas. I love granola, but I was always looking for a blend that reminded me of the tropics. This granola is big on taste, and I don't skimp on the yummy parts: the nuts and fruit.

4 c. old-fashioned rolled oats

2 c. sweetened shredded coconut

2 c. almonds, chopped

1 c. roasted unsalted cashews

1/2 c. canola oil

1/3 c. honey

1/2 tsp. ground cinnamon

1/4 tsp. nutmeg

1 c. dried mangoes, diced

1 c. dried cherries

1 c. dried pineapple

Preheat the oven to 350 degrees. Spray large sheet pan with nonstick cooking spray.

Toss the oats, coconut, almonds, cashews, and mangoes together in a large bowl. Whisk together the canola oil and honey. Add cinnamon and nutmeg to the oil mixture. Whisk till well combined. Pour honey/oil mixture over the oats and nuts. Stir till all of nuts, fruit, and oats are completely coated with the oil mixture. Pour onto a large sheet pan and spread evenly. Bake, stirring every 15 minutes until the mixture turns golden brown, about 25 to 30 minutes. Watch the baking granola closely because the coconut has a tendency to burn if it is not tossed often.

Remove the granola from the oven and allow to cool, stirring occasionally. Store the cooled granola in an airtight container for up to 6 months.

Kitchen Nugget: Feel free to play with the fruits and nuts. I change this up all the time. Sometimes I use apricots and dried blueberries, or other times I use dried figs and dried cherries. I have yet to find a combination I do not enjoy!

Southwest Egg Bake

If you love all things southwestern, then this is the egg bake for you. It is easy to make and packed with all the flavors you love.

10 large eggs
1/2 c. flour
1/2 tsp. baking powder
1 tsp. salt
1/4 c. butter (melted)
2 c. large curd cottage cheese
1/2 c. sour cream
2 c. Mexican-cheese blend, shredded
2 small can size green chilies
1 lb. chorizo sausage, cooked and crumbled

Preheat oven to 350 degrees. Coat a 9-x-13 pan with cooking spray. In a large bowl, whisk together eggs, salt, pepper, and baking powder. Add melted butter, cottage cheese, and sour cream. Whisk till well combined. Slowly fold in the shredded cheese, green chilies, and chorizo. Pour into the 9-x-13 pan. Place into oven and bake for 50 minutes or until set. Cut into squares and serve.

Serves: 12

Pasta, Rice, and Grains

I would be a liar if I told you this section doesn't make me giddy. It's no secret that I love carbohydrates in a deep and passionate way. These recipes are my tried-and-true favorites. In fact, my baked macaroni and cheese is the number one thing I take to friends and family when they are sick. If my mac and cheese can't heal your spirit, then it's time to see the doctor again.

In recent years, *comfort food* has become a "new" buzzword in cuisine. Frankly, I think the culinary world needed to check it before they wrecked it. There is nothing *new* about comfort foods. Down-home cooking is the root of America's culinary identity. Few things can warm your soul like a plate of shrimp and grits made with love.

One of my most humorous memories of cooking pasta is from my college years. For months I had bragged about my keen cooking skills and the awards I had won in high school, and now it was time for me to put up or shut up. I spent my entire week's food budget to buy the Italian smorgasbord I was going to prepare in my friend's kitchen. I cut, chopped, and simmered my sauce all to prepare the ultimate lasagna! I preheated the ancient-looking gas range and placed my labor of love (*and money!*) in the oven. Before I knew it, I heard an ungodly *boom* followed by a loud crash, and I rushed into the kitchen to find my lasagna lying on the floor next to the oven door, and the kitchen was filling with black smoke. The fire department arrived, and to my dismay I was informed that this kind of stove required me to light the pilot in the oven each (and every) time it was used.

Now come on…who ever heard of that?

Not me, not my lasagna, and certainly not the hungry friends looking at their meal on the floor. However, not all was lost. We still enjoyed an Italian feast that evening…thanks to the campus pizza joint!

Green Rice Casserole

Mom made this casserole every Easter alongside our ham. The dish even looks like spring! Filled with gorgeous white rice, green parsley, and the tart splash of lemon, you'll feel like you're eating a bit of spring in every bite.

3 c. cooked long grain rice
1 c. chopped parsley
1/2 c. grated Parmesan cheese
1 onion diced fine
1/4 c. diced fine green pepper
1 clove garlic minced
14 oz. can evaporated milk
2 eggs, beaten
1/2 c. canola oil
1 T. salt
1/2 tsp. seasoning salt
1/2 tsp. pepper
Juice of 1 lemon
Zest of 1 lemon

Preheat oven to 350 degrees, and spray a 2-quart casserole dish with cooking spray. Mix rice, parsley, cheese, onion, green peppers, and garlic in large bowl. In medium bowl, whisk together the milk, eggs, oil, lemon juice, lemon zest, and seasonings. Add rice to dish. Pour liquid mixture over the rice. Bake for 45 minutes or until custard consistency. Serve while warm.

Serves: 8

Love in a Pan Macaroni and Cheese

If this baked macaroni and cheese can't heal your illness, at least it will make your soul sing. This is the number one dish I prepare for my friends when they are sick or recovering from surgery. I have yet to meet anyone who does not rave about this dish! Perhaps it's the four cheeses, the creamy custard, or the comfort of noodles? Either way, smiles are always a guarantee.

    1 lb. elbow macaroni
    1 stick salted butter
    1/2 c. shredded Monterey Jack cheese
    1/2 c. shredded sharp cheddar cheese
    2 c. shredded Mexican cheese blend
    1 c. half-and-half
    1 c. heavy whipping cream
    8 oz. (1/2 of large block) Velveeta, cut into small cubes
    3 large eggs, lightly beaten
    1 tsp. seasoning salt
    1/8 tsp. freshly ground black pepper

Preheat the oven to 350 degrees. Lightly butter a deep 2 1/2-quart casserole.

Bring the large pot of salted water to a boil over high heat. Add the oil, then the elbow macaroni, and cook until the macaroni is just tender, about 7 minutes. Do not overcook! Drain well. Return to the cooking pot.

In a small saucepan, melt the butter. Stir into the macaroni. In a large bowl, mix the Monterey Jack cheese blend, and sharp cheddar. In a medium-sized bowl, whisk together the eggs, half-and-half, whipping cream, seasoning salt, and pepper. To the macaroni, add 1 1/2 cup of cheese mixture as well as the Velveeta cubes. Pour custard mixture over the macaroni. Transfer to the prepared casserole pan. Sprinkle with the remaining 1/2 cup of shredded cheese. Bake until it is bubbly and crisp around the edges, about 30-45 minutes. Remove from oven and serve hot.

Serves: 12

Kitchen Nugget: I always go ahead and make a double batch and freeze one of the two. I just add the custard mixture when I'm ready to take out and eat.

Potluck Macaroni Salad

This macaroni salad recipe makes enough to feed a small army. It's the perfect salad to take to a potluck or a picnic. My son often requests I make it at home where he will chow down on it all week long until the last salami is gone.

1 lb. pkg. salad macaroni (or ditali pasta)
1 c. celery, diced
1 c. red onion, diced
1 c. sharp cheddar, cubed into small bites
1 c. Swiss cheese, cubed into small bites
1/2 c. fresh Parmesan cheese, grated
1 c. dill pickles, diced
1 c. salami, diced
1 c. black olives, drained and diced or sliced
1/2 tsp. horseradish
1-2 T. garlic salt
1-2 T. fresh minced garlic
1/2 tsp. white pepper
1-2 tsp. fresh ground black pepper
1/2 tsp. cayenne pepper
1/2 tsp. dry mustard
1/2 tsp. celery salt
1 (3 oz.) jar diced pimentos, rinsed and drained
1-1 1/2 c. mayonnaise

Bring 2 quarts of water to a boil. Add macaroni, and cook until it is al dente, approximately 7-9 minutes. (*Do not overcook* the pasta or it will fall apart when the salad is tossed together!) Rinse macaroni until cool. Drain well, and let it dry for a spell. Place pasta in a large bowl.

Carefully fold in celery, onion, all of the cheeses, dill pickles, salami, and black olives. Refrigerate the pasta mixture, covered, overnight.

To make the sauce, mix the garlic salt, minced garlic, white pepper, black pepper, cayenne pepper, dry mustard, and celery salt together. Add mayonnaise and mix together. Add to the salad. Fold in pimentos. (You may use up to another 1/2 cup mayonnaise, if needed.) Refrigerate for at least 4 hours before serving.

Serves: 12

Savannah-Style Garlic Cheese Grits

After spending almost three weeks in beautiful Savannah, I became a huge fan of their favorite side dish: grits. This creamy, hearty dish with a garlic and cheese undertone is the epitome of Southern cooking. Now that I'm back in the Midwest, I continue to make this at least once a week for my family.

1 c. of uncooked grits (not instant)
2 (6 oz.) pkg. of Kraft garlic cheese spread (it's sold in a package that looks like a sausage link)
1/2 lb. applewood smoked bacon, cooked crisp (reserve drippings)
A dash of Tabasco
1/2 tsp. kosher salt
3/4 cup of unsalted butter
4 eggs
1/2 c. of half-and-half
1 c. sharp cheddar cheese, grated

Preheat oven to 350 degrees. Spray a large casserole dish with cooking spray.

Prepare the grits according to the package directions. While grits are still warm, stir in the cheese and butter. In a small bowl, beat the eggs, Tabasco, salt, and the half-and-half. Stir egg mixture into the grits. Pour into a lightly greased casserole dish. Bake for 40 minutes or until golden brown. Top with more grated cheddar and return to the oven until the cheese is melted. Serve warm.

Serves: 6

Easy Weeknight Spinach Alfredo

During the week, I'm always trying to plan a meal my family will be excited to eat. This alfredo is the perfect dish because of its restaurant quality and taste without the fuss. Feel free to add rotisserie chicken or shrimp to take it from a side dish to a full meal. Serve with a salad, and you've shown dinner who's boss!

    12 oz. frozen egg noodles
    1 (10-oz.) bag baby spinach
    3 T. unsalted butter
    3 T. all-purpose flour
    1 tsp. kosher salt
    1/4 tsp. freshly ground nutmeg
    1/8 tsp. freshly ground pepper
    2 c. milk (2% or higher)
    1/2 c. freshly grated Parmesan cheese, plus more for garnish if desired

Cook pasta in boiling water according to package directions. While pasta is cooking, in a heavy saucepan, melt butter over medium heat. Stir in flour, salt, nutmeg, and pepper until smooth. Cook and stir for 15-30 seconds or so. Gradually pour in milk, stirring constantly. Bring to a boil, stirring constantly; cook and stir for 2 minutes. Sauce will thicken as it stands.

Remove sauce from heat; stir in Parmesan cheese until melted; then stir in spinach. Drain cooked pasta in colander and return pasta to cooking pot. Pour spinach alfredo sauce into pasta, and stir until pasta is coated. Garnish with additional sprinkled Parmesan cheese if desired.

Serves: 4

Kitchen Nugget: This dish can be dressed up by adding rotisserie chicken, grilled shrimp, or lump crabmeat.

Curried Shrimp and Rice Salad

1 lb. extra-large (26-30 count) raw shrimp, shelled and de-veined

1 1/4 c. long grain or converted rice

1/2 box chicken stock

1 medium red onion, diced

1 medium red pepper, chopped

2 small jars marinated artichokes, drained (reserve the liquid for sauce)

1/2 jar green olives with pimiento, chopped

1 c. mayonnaise

1 tsp. curry powder

1/2 tsp. pepper

1 tsp. Old Bay seasoning

Cook rice according in package instructions. Allow to cool. In a large stockpot, boil shrimp with Old Bay seasoning. Cook till shrimp are tender and pink. Remove from water and place in an ice bath. Use a large bowl and place chopped onion, red pepper, artichokes, and olives. Add rice and toss till well combined. In small bowl, stir together mayonnaise, curry, and pepper. Add mayonnaise mixture to rice, and fold in till well combined. Chill for 4 hours and serve.

Serves: 6

Vegetable and Sides

Early on my mom taught me "a hungry child will not starve in the presence of food." Typically, this was when I was sitting at the dinner table stabbing my carrots and refusing to eat them. Later, when I would come to her and tell her I was hungry, I bet you can guess what she pulled out of the refrigerator: those dang carrots.

When I became a mother, I realized the wisdom in her message. If I feed my kids what I eat, they will grow up to be less picky and enjoy a variety of foods. And that is just what I did. If Jack and I were eating broccoli salad, they ate it too. Thankfully, both of my kids embraced this rule, and today they enjoy almost everything they try. Once, when one their friends came over and asked for something different, Caytie responded with, "You get what you get, and you don't throw a fit!" Their favorite is during the summertime when they request roasted beets, spaghetti squash, and heirloom tomatoes. Life is so much easier when you have a house filled with happy eaters!

Side dishes have changed back and forth through the years. I remember a time when Jack and I thought green bean casserole with mushroom soup was the epitome of cuisine. Today I try to make sides that start with as many fresh ingredients as possible and with only a hint of sauces where needed. Truly "tasting" vegetables is the fun part. However, don't get me wrong; this girl still loves a good ooey-gooey squash casserole!

I encourage everyone to really try and start to eat seasonally. Watch what's out in the market, and try to use those ingredients as your base. Eventually as the seasons pass, you'll begin to look forward to each one not only for the holidays but the produce they supply to your table!

Southern Creamed Corn

If you've ever traveled to the south, you've surely tasted the goodness that is creamed corn. I love the freshness of the corn along with the sweetness of the cream and the nutty flavor of Parmesan.

2 can size creamed corn
1 small bag frozen kernel corn or 6 fresh ears of corn, kernels removed
1 stick unsalted butter
4 slices of thick cut bacon, diced
1/2 tsp. kosher salt
1/2 tsp. black pepper
1/2 c. grated Parmesan cheese
1 c. half-and-half
1/4 c. sugar
1/2 c. water
1 T. cornstarch

In a large saucepan on medium heat, sauté bacon with butter till browned. Add frozen corn, sugar, and creamed corn. Heat till corn is warm throughout. Slowly add the half-and-half (*do not boil!*) Simmer. Add salt and pepper. Add cheese and stir till smooth.

To thicken: Mix water and cornstarch in separate bowl till smooth. Slowly add to the corn mixture and stir till thick. If the mixture becomes too thick, just add more half-and-half till it's the right consistency.

Serve warm with some extra grated Parmesan on top.

Serves: 6

Chipotle Grilled Asparagus

20 stalks fresh asparagus
3 T. olive oil
1/4 tsp. kosher salt
1 small block of Parmigiana Reggiano cheese, used to make shaved pieces
1 T. of extra virgin olive oil
1 T. balsamic vinegar

Spice Blend

1/2 tsp. fresh ground pepper
1/2 tsp. garlic powder
1/2 tsp. onion powder
1/2 tsp. paprika
1/2 tsp. chipotle powder
1/4 tsp. celery salt

Heat up grill to medium heat. While grill is heating, cut off woody end of the asparagus. Using a 9-x-13-inch pan, place asparagus in the pan. Sprinkle with olive oil, kosher salt, and 1 1/2 teaspoons of spice blend. Toss to coat evenly.

Place asparagus on grill and cook till grill marks appear, but do not burn. Flip asparagus to allow for even cooking. Once removed from the grill place on a platter, and pour balsamic over the spears and top with parmesan shavings. Serve while warm.

Serves: 5

Green Beans for the Soul

2 T. extra-virgin olive oil

8 thick-sliced hickory smoked bacon, chopped

1 large onion, chopped

1 Industrial-sized can green beans, drained

2 quarts chicken stock

1 tsp. minced garlic

1 tsp. kosher salt

1 tsp. freshly ground black pepper

1/4 tsp. red pepper flake

In a saucepan, add the olive oil, bacon, and onions, and cook on medium high heat until the onion is translucent and bacon is lightly crisp. Add drained green beans, chicken stock, and onion/bacon mixture to the slow cooker; season with salt and pepper. For a kick, add red pepper flakes! Taste and adjust seasoning. Simmer in Crock-Pot for 4 hours and then serve.

Serves: 12

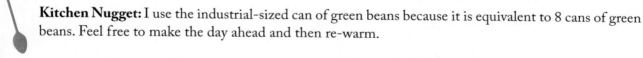

Kitchen Nugget: I use the industrial-sized can of green beans because it is equivalent to 8 cans of green beans. Feel free to make the day ahead and then re-warm.

Shaw Cranberry Slaw

This slaw recipe is from my uncle Phil's side of the family. At first glance I was a bit freaked out by the cranberries, but after one bite I am a fan. I love the freshness of the crisp cabbage with the sneaky hint of sweet and tart from the dried cranberries. Truly a dish you have to taste to appreciate.

5 c. cabbage, shredded
1 1/2 c. dried cranberry
1/2 c. green onion chopped
1/2 c. green pepper chopped

Dressing

1/2 c. mayonnaise
1 T. sweet relish
1 T. honey mustard
1 T. honey
1/2 tsp. salt
1/2 tsp. pepper

In a large bowl, combine the cabbage, cranberries, green onion, and green pepper. In a smaller bowl, mix together the mayonnaise, sweet relish, honey mustard, honey, salt, and pepper. Stir until well combined. Add slaw dressing to veggies and toss. Refrigerate for at least 4-6 hours before serving.

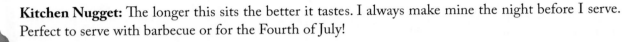

Kitchen Nugget: The longer this sits the better it tastes. I always make mine the night before I serve. Perfect to serve with barbecue or for the Fourth of July!

Chilled Bean Salad

2 c. french cut green beans, drained
1 can Le Seur peas, drained (canned peas in the silver can)
1 can corn, drained
1 c. sugar
1/2 c. vegetable oil
2/3 c. cider vinegar
1 tsp. salt
1 tsp. pepper
1 green pepper, chopped fine
1 red onion, chopped fine
1 small jar pimento, drained and chopped
3 celery ribs, chopped fine

In a large colander drain the green beans, peas, corn and pimento. Once it is well drained, place canned items in a large plastic bowl and set aside. Using a medium-sized saucepan over medium heat combine the sugar, oil, vinegar, salt and pepper. Bring to a boil and then remove from heat and allow to cool completely.

Add the fresh cut veggies to the bowl of canned veggies. Pour the cooled dressing over the veggies. Gently toss together. Cover and chill overnight before serving.

Serves: 8

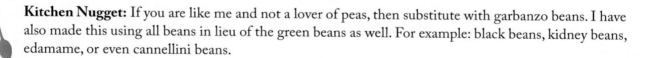

Kitchen Nugget: If you are like me and not a lover of peas, then substitute with garbanzo beans. I have also made this using all beans in lieu of the green beans as well. For example: black beans, kidney beans, edamame, or even cannellini beans.

Grandma's Waldorf Salad

This salad is the one I had to make in the middle of the night when I was pregnant with Jackson. I tried skimping and making a knockoff of my Grandma's classic but my tummy and baby knew the difference. Sometimes the real deal is the only way to go…

3 chopped Granny Smith Apples, cored and seeded
1 c. celery, chopped fine
1/2 c. pecans, toasted and chopped
1/2 fresh lemon juice
1 egg, separated yolk and white
1 c. sugar
1 T. flour
1 c. vinegar

Place the chopped apples, celery, and pecans in a medium-sized plastic bowl. Toss apples with lemon juice and set aside.

To make the dressing, beat the egg yolk in a small bowl. Add to a small saucepan along with the sugar/flour mixture as well as the vinegar. Heat over low heat stirring constantly with a whisk until thickened. Remove from heat. Beat egg white with an electric mixer till steady peaks are reached. Fold in egg whites to the cooled vinegar/sugar mixture. To thin out this cream mixture feel free to add a tablespoon at a time of whipping cream. Add the dressing to the fresh apple mixture and serve!

Quickie Au Gratin Potatoes

This little gem came about when my kids were begging for potoatoes and if I mashed them one more time I might just just come "un-glued". (Momma speak for not good.) So, this is what I came up with and I have to say now it is a weekly favorite! Feel free to experiment with the ingredients! It is very forgiving!

1 pkg. frozen Southern Style Hash Browns
1 onion, chopped fine
1/2 stick butter, unsalted
1 can reduced cream of chicken soup
1/2 c. sour cream
1/2 c. Philadelphia Cooking Creme, original flavor
2 c. Cheddar cheese, grated
salt and pepper
1 c. canned fried onions
1 c. corn flakes

Preheat oven to 350 degrees and spray a 9-×-13-inch casserole pan with nonstick spray. In a small skillet sauté onion and butter till tender. Remove from heat. Using a large bowl, pour in hash browns, onion mixture, cream of chicken soup, sour cream, cooking creme, and shredded cheese. Stir together until well combined. Add in salt and pepper to taste. Pour potato mixture into the casserole pan. Combine corn flakes and fried onions in a bowl. Sprinkle on top of casserole. Bake for 30 minutes covered with foil. Remove foil and allow to cook 15 additional minutes or until topping is browned. Serve!

Kitchen Nugget: I have added diced ham or chopped bacon for a heartier dish. This is also fantastic if you add green chilis and mexi cheese for a South of the Border side dish.

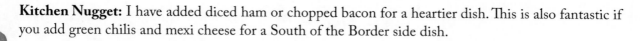

Summer Squash Casserole

During summers when I was a kid, I was constantly opening the front door to find a large paper sack filled with squash. Our neighbors would leave it because they knew the Walker household could eat some squash! This was my favorite thing my Mom would make for summertime dinners. Creamy and delicate all while thinking you are being healthy!

4 yellow squash cut in half and sliced into 1/4 inch slices

1 sweet yellow onion, chopped

4 slices thick cut applewood smoked bacon, chopped

1/2 c. cheese whiz

8 oz. sour cream

1 sleeve Ritz Crackers, crushed

Preheat oven to 350 degrees. Spray a 9-x-13-inch casserole pan with nonstick cooking spray and set aside. Sauté onions and bacon till it is translucent and bacon is crisp. Drain fat and remove onions and bacon and place into a large bowl. Add in squash and toss together. In a small bowl, mix together the cheese whiz and sour cream. Pour cheese mixure into squash and mix together and place into the casserole pan. Place crushed Ritz crackers on top and bake for 30 minutes until crispy.

Kitchen Nugget: This dish works great with ANY squash. Do not discriminate and have fun experimenting. I also enjoy placing these in individual ramekins to bake them in for a more fancy serving style at an adult cookout!

Pan Roasted Brussels Sprouts

Bless these little veggies' hearts! They are the most mistreated veggie I know of and the sad part is that they are DELICIOUS! Just STOP BOILING them! I re-created this recipe after traveling to the Northern California coast and having the best brussels sprouts of my life. You might call it a Brussels Sprout Renaissance! So give these a whirl and I promise you will never mistreat those little guys ever again!

2 lb. fresh brussels sprouts, trimmed and cut in half

1/4 lb. applewood smoked bacon, cut into pieces

1/2 Vidalia onion, chopped

3 T. olive oil

1/4 c. dried cranberries

1/2 c. pecans, roasted and rough chopped

4 oz. goat cheese, crumbled

sea salt and pepper

Preheat oven to 425 degrees and place brussels sprouts, bacon, Vidalia onion and olive oil in a medium-sized bowl. Toss till well coated. Sprinkle with sea salt and pepper. Place on a well-greased roasting pan and put in oven. Roast for 25 minutes or until brussels sprouts are are fork tender. Remove pan and allow to cool slightly. Toss brussels sprouts, cranberries and pecans together. Place in a serving bowl and top with crumbled goat cheese.

Moo, Cluck, and Oink

Growing up in Oklahoma, I was blessed to be fed some of the best beef, chicken, and pork around. There are a lot of great things the Midwest does not have, but meat is certainly not one of them. I can't think of anything more delicious to this sassy mama than a grilled burger, fried chicken and waffles, or a succulent pork roast.

However, there is a special place in my heart for my number one favorite meat: bacon! This slab of love is the top dog of all things pork. My husband once told me, "Bacon is a pig's way of saying 'I love you.'" If that's true, I promise the next time I'm at a petting zoo to kiss that pig right on his lovely pink snout. Needless to say, you can put bacon on nearly anything, and I'm a happy gal.

When cooking with meat, I encourage you to get the best cut of meat you can afford. I remember times when Jack sent me to the store with $10 and told me to buy enough chicken for the week. That meant I got that big bag of leg quarters that was typically $5 and required you to pick through it carefully as not to miss any leftover feathers. Yes, I said it. Feathers!

Many times cheaper meat means more cut corners, and those corners are in the butchering department. But I more than made do with what we could afford. With some yummy spices and marinades, no one was ever the wiser!

I also learned that shopping for a roast can leave one feeling overwhelmed by all the options. Chuck, rump, rib, butt–which one is best? I quickly learned the best choice was to talk with your store's butcher. I would tell them the type of dish I wanted to make, and they would be all too happy to suggest the type of roast I should use.

One of my favorite parts of cooking with meat is experimenting with spices. For the following recipes, I have suggested some common spices that, when combined, will make a sensational rub or seasoning. It will transform a boring cut of meat from ho-hum to mouthwatering!

Curry Chicken Salad

This is one of my most requested recipes. It began with a recipe I borrowed from a girlfriend, and then I added a touch of sassy to it. It's a perfect salad to make for a luncheon or to take on a camping trip. I often make it in bulk and eat on it all week!

5 boneless skinless chicken breasts (roasted and cubed)
4 tsp. olive oil
1/2 tsp. kosher salt
1/2 tsp. ground pepper
1/2 tsp. thyme
4 green onions, chopped
1 c. celery chopped
3/4 c. red grapes, cut in half
1/2 c. pecans or walnuts, chopped
1 c. mayonnaise
3 T. honey
1 1/2 tsp. curry powder

Preheat oven to 375 degrees.

To roast chicken breasts, place chicken breasts on a cookie sheet. Drizzle with olive oil. Sprinkle with salt, pepper, and thyme. Place in oven and bake for 30 minutes. Allow to cool completely. Cut into cubes. In a large bowl, add chicken, onions, celery, grapes, and nuts. In a small bowl, whisk together the mayonnaise, honey, curry, salt, and pepper. Stir till smooth. Add dressing to chicken mixture. Stir till well combined. Cover and chill until ready to serve.

Gigi's Warm Chicken Salad

This is my family's favorite chicken casserole. It comes from Donella Amis, aka Gigi, and she serves it every year at her cookie exchange party in December. I look forward to the party just so I can get a hug from "Gigi" herself and taste that delicious casserole! After many months of pleading, she has given me her blessing to share her recipe with the world. She truly is a grand dame of sassiness that I aspire to be one day!

4 boneless/skinless chicken breast, boiled and cubed

1 c. chopped celery

1 onion, chopped fine

1/2 c. unsalted butter

1 c. mayonnaise

1 can size cream of chicken soup

1 small jar pimentos, drained

1 c. Lays potato chips, crumbled

1 c. cheddar cheese, shredded

1/2 tsp. kosher salt

1/2 tsp. fresh ground pepper

Preheat oven to 350 degrees. Boil the chicken breasts. Remove from water and allow to cool. Then chop into bite-sized pieces. Place chicken in a large bowl, and add all the other ingredients. Place in sprayed 9-x-13-inch baking dish. Top with crumbled Lays potato chips and cheddar cheese. Cook for 30 minutes till warm and bubbly. Serve alone or over egg noodles.

Serves: 8

Family Night Goulash

This super easy dish has been a staple in homes for decades! Soon after we got married, Jack requested goulash. I had never heard of it so, to my rescue was my father-in-law with this south-side classic! My kids request this hearty ground beef and noodle dinner every week. Luckily, I don't have to feel bad because it's loaded with veggies!

2 lb. ground beef

1 lb. elbow macaroni

2 tsp. olive oil

1 green pepper, chopped

1 onion, chopped

1 large can size tomato soup

1 large can size crushed tomatoes

2 tsp. Italian seasoning

1/4 c. brown sugar

1/2 tsp. ground nutmeg

2 c. cheddar cheese

Brown ground beef and drain. Set aside. Bring a large pot of water to a boil. Add noodles. Cook till al dente. Drain and set aside.

In a large stockpot over medium heat, sauté onions and green peppers in the olive oil. Add Italian seasonings and ground beef. Allow to cook until the meat is browned. Drain grease and return to stockpot to finish sauce. To make sauce, add green peppers and onions till mixed well, and then add the tomato soup, crushed tomatoes, brown sugar, and nutmeg. Allow sauce to cook on medium heat till it simmers. Stir in the al dente noodles. Serve in bowls, and top with grated cheddar cheese.

Slow Cooker French Dip with Horseradish Aioli

This is the meal I make when I need to feed a group of hungry boys. It's also perfect to serve to your family on a busy weeknight. Perfectly cooked in the slow cooker, and best of all, the *au jus* is in there too.

   4 lb. rump roast or beef tenderloin
   2 (10.5 oz.) can beef broth, low sodium
   2 (10.5 oz.) can condensed French onion soup
   1 (12 fluid oz.) can or bottle beer
   6-8 soft hoagie rolls
   1 tsp. horseradish
   1/2 c. mayonnaise
   6 slices provolone cheese

Trim excess fat from the rump roast or beef tenderloin, and place in a slow cooker. Add the beef broth, onion soup, and beer. Cook on the low setting for 7 hours.

Preheat oven to 350 degrees.

To prepare horseradish aioli: In a small bowl, combine mayonnaise and horseradish. Stir till well combined.

Split French rolls and spread with horseradish mayo. Top with provolone cheese. Bake 10 minutes or until heated through and cheese is melted.

Remove meat from slow cooker and allow to rest on a cutting board for 10 minutes. Either slice meat or shred into bite-sized pieces and place on the warm rolls. Use the leftover juices in the slow cooker as the au jus or dipping sauce. Place into small bowls, and serve with sandwich.

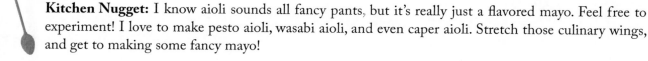

Kitchen Nugget: I know aioli sounds all fancy pants, but it's really just a flavored mayo. Feel free to experiment! I love to make pesto aioli, wasabi aioli, and even caper aioli. Stretch those culinary wings, and get to making some fancy mayo!

Lil' Ranch Sliders

This is my take on my favorite burger in the world! It's from a bar in Norman, Oklahoma, and I have loved it since my college days. All I've done is reduced the size of the burger and used my mama's homemade ranch dressing. Then I went over the top with it and added smoky cheddar and bacon.

1 1/2 lb. of 80/20 ground chuck

2 T. grated onion, juice and all

1/2 tsp. sea salt

1/2 tsp. fresh ground pepper

1/2 tsp. Worcestershire sauce

6-8 slices smoked cheddar

6-8 slices applewood smoked bacon, cooked crisp

1/4 c. butter, melted

6-8 mini burger buns

1/2 c. of This Ain't No Hidden Valley Ranch Dressing (see appetizer section)

Preheat grill to medium high heat. In a large bowl, combine ground chuck, grated onion, sea salt, pepper, and Worcestershire sauce. Form 6-8 small patties. Do not overmix or press the meat. Place on grill and allow to cook 4 to 5 minutes or until crust forms. Flip over and allow that side to brown. *Do not double flip* or *press*. The juice is how your burgers stay juicy!

While burgers are cooking, butter buns and place on grill to warm. A few minutes before removing burgers from grill, top with bacon and a cheese slice. Cook till cheese is melted. Remove buns and burgers from heat, and allow to rest for 10 minutes.

Put burger patties on buns and top with 2 tablespoons homemade Ranch dressing. Place on a large platter and serve!

Serves: 6-8 mini burgers

Chicken Bruschetta with Balsamic Glaze

In the spring and early summer, I love to make this dish. It reminds me of a warm summer day in Italy with fresh tomatoes, basil, and mozzarella. My kind of heaven in one easy 9-x-13-inch pan. I promise your family will fall in love with this fresh dish!

1/2 c. all purpose flour

2 eggs, slightly beaten

4 boneless skinless chicken breasts

1/4 c. grated Parmesan cheese

1/2 tsp. kosher salt

1/4 tsp. freshly ground pepper

1/4 c. Panko bread crumbs

1 T. butter, melted

2 large tomatoes, seeded and chopped

3 T. minced fresh basil

3 T. capers

2 garlic cloves, minced

1 T. olive oil

3 T. pre-made balsamic glaze

Preheat oven to 375 degrees. Place flour and eggs in separate bowls. Dip chicken in flour and then dredge in beaten eggs. Place in a greased 9-x-13-inch baking dish. Combine the Parmesan cheese, Panko crumbs, and butter. Sprinkle over chicken. Cover baking dish with foil. Bake for 25 minutes. Remove foil; continue to bake 5-10 minutes longer or until top is browned.

While chicken is baking, in a small bowl, combine the remaining ingredients. Spoon over the chicken. Return to the oven for 3-5 minutes or until tomato mixture is heated through. Drizzle chicken with balsamic glaze, and serve with buttered angel hair pasta.

Serves: 4

Slow Cooker Pork Roast with Cranberries

The creation of that little self-contained hot pot has saved many a working woman and mama. Thank goodness for the Crock-Pot! Pork roast slow-cooked till tender with a warm cranberry glaze makes for a happy plate any evening in my house. The best part is you throw it all in the pot before you race out the door in the morning.

2-3 lb. lean pork loin

1 tsp. kosher salt

1/2 tsp. freshly ground black pepper

2 T. olive oil

1 (15 oz.) can whole berry cranberry sauce

3 oz. pineapple juice

2 T. cider vinegar

1 T. Dijon mustard

2 T. honey

1/2 tsp. cinnamon

1 T. cornstarch

3 tsp. cold water

Rub salt and black pepper onto pork loin and place in a large skillet with olive oil over high heat. Sear the outside of the pork loin till crust forms, approximately 2-3 minutes per side. Place directly into slow cooker. Add cranberry sauce, pineapple juice, vinegar, Dijon mustard, honey, and cinnamon. Cook on low for 5-6 hours.

Mix cornstarch and water in small bowl, and add last 15 minutes of cooking time. This will help make the cranberry glaze! Remove loin and place onto a serving plate. Allow to rest 5 minutes. Slice into 1/2-inch slices. Serve!

Kitchen Nugget: This recipe goes perfect with quinoa, buttered potatoes, or noodles.

Cuban Pork Roast with Mojo Sauce

When we're in Florida on the boat, we eat Cuban at least three times a week. I love the flavors of their slow-roasted meats. It's a combination of citrus fruits, garlic, and vinegar. Amazing.

  2-4 lb. pork butt or picnic
  1 large onion, sliced
  1 (4 oz.) jar minced garlic
  1 tsp. kosher salt
  1 tsp. freshly ground pepper
  2 tsp. oregano
  1 c. of bitter orange juice
  1/2 c. olive oil

Preheat oven to 350 degrees. In a small bowl, combine minced garlic, salt, pepper, and olive oil. Mix together, and then rub into meat on all sides and in every little crevice. Put pork into a large roasting pan, and place the sliced onion all around. Pour orange juice on top of meat. Cook 2 hours uncovered. Cover with foil, and cook 2 more hours. Uncover and cook 90 minutes more. Let set for 30 minutes, and then shred with a fork.

Serve with yellow rice and black beans. Hello, Havana!

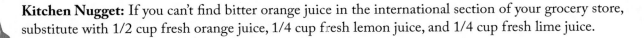

Kitchen Nugget: If you can't find bitter orange juice in the international section of your grocery store, substitute with 1/2 cup fresh orange juice, 1/4 cup fresh lemon juice, and 1/4 cup fresh lime juice.

Naughty Trucker Grilled Cheese Sandwich

My recipe was featured in *Rachael Ray Magazine* in May 2011. I've been making this for years, and my family loves it each and every time! This sandwich is simple yet huge on flavor.

2 slices country white bread

1/4 c. sharp cheddar cheese, grated

3 oz. oven roasted turkey breast

2 strips of thick cut bacon

Olive oil

1/4 c. caramelized onions

2 T. salted butter, softened

This Ain't No Hidden Valley Ranch dressing, see appetizer section

Preheat a cast iron skillet on medium high heat. Cut onion in half and slice. Add to hot skillet, and top with olive oil. Cook slowly till golden and caramelized. Place 1 tablespoon of Ranch dressing on both slices of bread; then add grated cheese to each piece of bread. Put turkey slices on one piece of bread, and top with caramelized onions. Place pieces of bread together, and butter both sides. Add to hot skillet, and cook until toasty and the cheese is melted.

Mama's Chicken and Green Chili Waffles

If you are missing your mama and need some comfort, this is the recipe for you. I love to make this meal on Sunday nights. The batter I use on my chicken is light and crunchy with tons of flavor. Then place it on top of a sweet corn and green chili waffle, and top with warm maple syrup. I can think of no better way to start the week than with this meal!

1 lb. chicken tenders
2 T. all purpose flour
1/2 tsp. cornstarch
1 tsp. kosher salt
1/2 tsp. seasoning salt
1/2 tsp. ground pepper
1/4 tsp. onion powder
1/4 tsp. powdered sugar
1/8 tsp. Spanish paprika
Corn or vegetable oil, for deep-fryer
1/2 tsp. powdered egg whites
3 T. half-and-half

Waffles

1 3/4 c. cornmeal
3/4 c. all-purpose flour
1 T. baking powder
1 tsp. salt
1 T. sugar
1 large egg
1 1/2 c. whole milk
1 c. canned cream-style corn
1 small can (4 oz.) chopped mild green chili peppers
5 T. melted butter

Preheat your deep fryer to 375 degrees. In a mixing bowl, blend egg whites and milk with a wire whisk till frothy. Measure dry ingredients into a gallon-sized re-sealable bag, close, and shake well to mix.

Soak chicken tenders in milk and egg bath. Remove and place into plastic bag with dried ingredients. Close and shake till chicken is completely covered. Carefully place coated chicken into hot oil, and cook till golden brown and juices run clear. Remove from oil, and drain on a plate lined with paper towels.

To make waffle batter, in a medium bowl, combine cornmeal, flour, baking powder, salt, and sugar. In a small bowl, whisk together the eggs with milk. Then stir in the creamed corn and green chilies. Combine the two mixtures, stirring just until blended. Stir in the melted butter.

Bake waffles in a preheated and oiled waffle iron until crispy. Set aside in a warmed oven till ready to serve. To serve your chicken and waffles, simply place your warm crispy waffle on a plate, top with chicken strips, and pour over warm maple syrup.

Serves: 6

No B.S. Ribs with Sassy Sauce

If you love ribs but hate thinking about baby sitting the smoker all day, well then this is the recipe for you! Thank you to Bill Shuler for bringing these amazing ribs into my life. You might say this recipe caused a grilling renaissance in my life. Boil rather than smoking! Sounds crazy but you cannot dismiss the results!

3 lbs. pork baby back ribs
1/2 tsp. garlic salt
1/2 tsp. fresh ground pepper
1 tsp. liquid smoke

Sassy Sauce

1 c. ketchup
1/4 c. Dijon mustard
1/2 c. brown sugar
1/2 tsp. garlic salt
1/2 tsp. fresh ground pepper
1/2 c. molasses
1 tsp. liquid smoke
2 tsp. Worcestershire sauce
1/8 tsp. cayenne pepper

Cut each rack of ribs into 3 rib sections. Place ribs in a large a large stock pot filled with water making sure to cover them with at least 1 inch of water. Add in the garlic salt, pepper and liquid smoke. Bring to a boil then reduce heat to a slow simmer for 1 hour. Remove ribs from water and place on a large platter.

To prepare the barbecue sauce: Place ketchup, Dijon mustard and brown sugar in a medium-sized saucepan. Add in the remaining ingredients and simmer over medium heat for about 15 minutes. Remove from heat.

How to grill ribs: After ribs have boiled, place on either a gas or charcoal grill for approximately 30 minutes at low heat. Turn ribs and baste with sauce, being careful not to allow sauce to burn. Remove from heat and serve with extra sauce.

Lemon Herb Brick Chicken

This recipe is one that I love to share. It sounds too good to be true! All you need is a big cast iron pan and a brick. Simply delicious and perfect to serve for a family dinner or for guests!

3-4 lbs. whole chicken
2 1/2 T. fresh thyme, chopped
2 T. fresh rosemary, chopped
1 lemon, zested
6 garlic cloves peeled & smashed
1/4 c. olive oil
sea salt and pepper

Rinse the chicken in cold water and pat dry. Remove the backbone of chicken to create 2 large halves of chicken. Dry the chicken halves completely. Combine the thyme, rosemary, garlic, lemon zest and olive oil in a large zip-top bag or mixing bowl. DO NOT SALT CHICKEN NOW! This makes for a tough bird! Add the chicken halves. Zip and refrigerate overnight (or for at least 4 hours).

Heat the oven to 450 degrees. Wrap two bricks in a couple of layers of foil.

Remove the chicken from the refrigerator and sprinkle with salt and pepper. Set a large cast-iron or other heavy ovenproof pan over medium-high heat. When hot, add just enough vegetable oil to lightly film the pan. Put the chicken halves, skin side down, in the pan and immediately put a brick on top of each half. Turn the heat to medium and cook until the skin is a deep golden brown. (about 20 to 25 minutes) Remove the bricks, turn the chicken halves over (skin side up), and put the pan in the hot oven to finish roasting the chicken another 20 to 25 minutes. Once chicken is done, remove from the oven and allow chicken to rest 10 minutes before serving.

The Sweet Stuff

Many people like to feel guilty about dessert. I am most certainly *not* one of those people. I believe with all of my heart that life is short, so eat dessert first.

I learned this lesson after losing my mom very suddenly in 2004. It may sound strange, but I decided that when she got to heaven she probably didn't think to herself, *I never should have had that piece of key lime pie yesterday.* Today I see every day as a gift and as a potential blessing. The same applies to how I feel about desserts. I'm not saying one should eat an entire key lime pie every other day, but I do believe a little sweet treat never killed anyone.

I hope you enjoy the following recipes as much as I do. As I mentioned in an earlier chapter, baking is way for me to relieve stress and get back on track. I love the feeling of opening my kitchen windows to cool a pie or the delicious smell of warm brownies wafting through the house. In fact, my husband's associates will often ask him, "Does your house always smell like cupcakes?" Needless to say, my friends and neighbors love when I am stressed! They get all kinds of sweet treats sent their direction when I'm in the midst of some good baking therapy. Trust me; it's cheaper than a psychiatrist, and in the end, it makes a lot more people happy!

The following are some of my best kitchen nuggets for desserts:

- Use whole milk when a recipe calls for milk. The fat and cream will make for a more delicate, rich cake.

- Only use unsalted butter. Most desserts call for salt in the recipe, and you don't want to double up.

- I *love* vanilla paste! The paste is simply vanilla beans that have been scraped and then mixed together with corn syrup. The small seeds really intensify the flavor. This product can be used exactly as vanilla extract and is a sure-fire way to make your frostings and baked goods have a much richer vanilla flavor.

- Invest in parchment paper. I use it to line my pans, counters, or anything when I'm baking or cooking desserts. This paper will keep your baked goods from overbrowning and sticking.

- If you're looking for new cookie sheets, check your local restaurant supply store or warehouse club. The industrial half sheets are what the pros use, and they're a fraction of the cost of those you find in a gourmet store.

- Use eggs at room temperature. This helps the batter to stay the same temperature and will allow your eggs to incorporate better. Fuller, fluffier, happier eggs will make for a better dessert in the end.

All of these tips are ones that I have found to be 100-percent true. I've had many a failure, but many times it was because I tried to skimp or skip a step. Haste makes waste, and who in the world would want to waste something as delicious as dessert?

Pots de Créme

This recipe sounds hoity-toity, but my hubby calls them "pudding pots," and that pretty much sums it up. If you want to impress the chocolate lover in your life without spending all day in the kitchen, this is the recipe for you!

> 1 1/2 c. heavy whipping cream
> 1/2 c. Kahlua liqueur
> 1/2 tsp. vanilla or vanilla paste
> 6 oz. bittersweet chocolate, chopped into small pieces
> 6 large egg yolks
> 1 T. sugar
> 1/4 tsp. salt
> Whipped cream (optional), to garnish

Preheat oven to 300 degrees. Add chopped chocolate to a blender. Heat cream and a pinch of salt in a small pot until it just comes to a boil. Pour the hot cream over the chocolate, and blend until melted and smooth. Let cool slightly; then blend in the Kahlua liqueur and vanilla.

Whisk together the egg yolks and sugar in a separate bowl. Slowly blend chocolate, and add in egg and sugar mixture. Continue to blend till completely combined.

Pour the custard mixture evenly into 8 (4-5 oz.) ramekins or small teacups. Place the dishes into a deep pan, and fill pan with hot water until halfway up the sides of the ramekins. Tightly cover with aluminum foil poked with a few holes. Bake until custard is set around edges but still slightly liquid in center (about 35-45 minutes). Custard will become firmer as it cools.

Remove pots de crème from water bath, remove foil, and let cool at room temperature for about an hour. Transfer to refrigerator, and cool completely overnight. Serve with a dollop of whipped cream, and sprinkle with cocoa powder on top.

Devilish Brownies

Okay...I'm going to say it. These brownies are out of this world and maybe one of the best things I make. I'm begged for the recipe every time I bring to a party or function. These are super chocolaty with a fudge-like consistency. Once you taste these, you will never make those boxed brownies ever again.

4 oz. unsweetened chocolate, chopped

2 oz. bittersweet chocolate chips

1 lb. plus 2 c. semisweet chocolate chips

1 lb. unsalted butter

7 eggs

1 T. instant coffee granules

2 T. vanilla paste

2 1/4 c. sugar

1 T. baking powder

1 tsp. kosher salt

1 1/4 c. all-purpose flour, divided

3 c. pecans or walnuts

Preheat oven to 350 degrees. Line a 13-x-18-x-1.5-inch sheet pan with parchment paper. Spray well with nonstick spray.

In a medium-sized saucepan on low heat, melt unsweetened and bittersweet chocolate and 1 pound of semisweet chocolate chips with butter. Once it is melted, remove from heat and cool slightly.

In a small bowl, combine the remaining 2 cups of chocolate chips and 1/4 cup flour. Set aside. This technique keeps the chocolate chips suspended in the batter and keeps it from settling on the bottom of the pan while baking.

In a medium-sized bowl, combine 1 cup of flour and the baking powder. Using a large bowl, mix together the eggs, sugar, coffee granules, salt, and vanilla paste. Slowly add a small amount of chocolate mixture to the eggs. Once combined, add the remaining chocolate, and stir well. Add the flour and baking powder mixture, and mix only till incorporated. Do not overmix! Add in chocolate chips and 1/4 cup. Stir once again only to combine. Add nuts. Once mixed, pour into the greased pan. Tap tray on counter to remove air bubbles.

Bake in oven for 30 minutes. Rotate pan halfway through baking time. Cool completely. Chill overnight in refrigerator. To cut, remove parchment sling and cut into squares.

Mama's Sugar Cookies

This is the first cookie my babies ever ate. It's perfect because it's not loaded with sugar and is firm. The best thing about this cookie is that it works beautifully for decorating. It's a firm, sturdy cookie with a hint of lemon.

> 1/2 c. unsalted butter, room temperature
> 1 c. sugar
> 2 eggs
> 1 tsp. vanilla or vanilla paste
> 1/2 tsp. lemon extract
> 2 1/2 c. all purpose flour
> 3 tsp. baking powder
> 1/2 tsp. salt

Cream together the butter and sugar till fluffy. Add eggs one at a time, and beat into butter mixture. Add in vanilla and lemon extract. In a small bowl, combine the flour, baking powder, and salt. Slowly add flour mixture to butter, and mix till dough comes together. Divide dough into 2 portions. Flatten into a disc, and place in fridge for one hour.

To roll out: lightly flour workspace and then place disc on flour and roll till about 1/4-inch thick. Use cookie cutters to cut out. Place on parchment paper-lined baking sheet. Return leftover dough to refrigerator till ready to roll again. (This keeps them from spreading while baking.)

Bake cookies in a 350-degree oven for about 10 minutes. The time may differ depending on the size of your cookie. The best way to tell doneness is to bake until edges are light brown. Cool completely, and then decorate! I like to use royal icing or dip in melted semisweet chocolate.

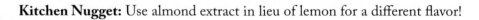

Kitchen Nugget: Use almond extract in lieu of lemon for a different flavor!

Sunday's Chocolate Chip Cookies

I have to give it up to my sister. She's a phenomenal mother of two boys with autism, and she still finds the time to make these chocolate chip cookies every week for her family. This is my all-time favorite cookie, and they taste just like those you'd buy in a bakery.

1 stick unsalted butter, melted
1/2 c. butter-flavored Crisco, melted
3/4 c. granulated sugar
3/4 c. light brown sugar
2 large eggs
2 T. real vanilla extract or vanilla paste
1 tsp. baking soda
1/2 tsp. salt
3 c. all purpose flour (may need 2-4 T. more if dough seems too loose)
1 1/2 c. semisweet chocolate chips
1 c. pecans, chopped (optional)

Preheat oven to 375 degrees. Line cookie sheets with parchment paper or use a Silpat baking sheet. In a large bowl, completely melt the butter and Crisco in the microwave until liquefied. Using an electric mixer, combine sugars and butter mixture in bowl and mix well. On medium speed, mix in eggs until completely incorporated. Add vanilla to sugar mixture.

In a large bowl, mix together the baking soda, salt, and flour. On slow speed, add flour one cup at a time until it is all added. Add chocolate chips and nuts, stirring until combined.

Drop cookie dough onto a baking pan using a large ice cream scoop (this way nobody can fight over who has the bigger cookie!) and bake at 375 degrees for 12-15 minutes. Remove from oven and allow to cool. Store leftover cookies in an airtight container.

Serves: 1 1/2 dozen large cookies

Mile-High Peanut Butter Pie

I make this pie all summer long. It's creamy, rich, and tastes like a chilled Reese's Peanut Butter Cup. If you have a peanut butter lover in your house, I guarantee they will love it.

    6 oz. premade Oreo piecrust
    1 c. semisweet chocolate chips
    1-8 oz. pkg. cream cheese, softened
    3/4 c. creamy peanut butter
    3/4 c. powdered sugar plus 1 T.
    2 c. heavy whipping cream plus 2 T.
    1 tsp. vanilla or vanilla paste
    1/4 c. mini chocolate chips
    1/4 c. chopped peanuts

In a small bowl, melt chocolate chips with 2 tablespoons whipping cream in a microwave. Pour inside Oreo crust, and spread all over the inside and on the bottom. Set in fridge for 30 minutes to set.

Using a large bowl that has been chilled in the freezer for 15 minutes, whip the heavy whipping cream with vanilla and 1 tablespoon powdered sugar till stiff peaks form.

In a large bowl, use a hand mixer and blend together the cream cheese and peanut butter. Mix in the powdered sugar. Using a spatula, fold in the 3/4 of the whipped cream. Spread peanut butter filling inside piecrust and top with whipping cream. Garnish with mini chocolate chips and chopped peanuts. Cover pie loosely with plastic wrap and place into the freezer. Allow to chill for 4-8 hours.

Before serving: allow pie to sit on counter for 10 minutes and then cut with a warm knife. Serve immediately!

Key Lime Pie

Every Mother's Day my husband makes this pie for me. It's my most favorite dessert in the world. I love the crisp buttery crust coupled with the super tart lime flavor. The best part of all is the vanilla bean whipped cream.

1 sleeve of graham crackers (1/3 of box)

1/2 c. melted unsalted butter

1/3 c. sugar

1/4 c. pecans, chopped fine

3 egg yolks

Zest of 2 limes

1 (14 oz. can) sweetened condensed milk

2/3 c. key lime juice

1 1/2 c. heavy whipping cream, chilled

2 T. confectioners' sugar

1 tsp. vanilla paste

Preheat the oven to 350 degrees. Butter a 9-inch pie pan. Crush the graham crackers; place in a food processor and process till course crumbs (not dust). If you do not have a food processor, place graham crackers in a large Ziploc and crush using a rolling pin. In a large bowl, add the melted butter, pecans, and sugar. Stir till combined. Press the mixture into the bottom and sides of the pie pan. Bake the crust until set and golden brown, for 8 minutes. Set aside; leave the oven on.

Meanwhile as the shell is baking, in an electric mixer with the wire whisk attachment, beat the egg yolks and lime zest until creamy and very fluffy, about 5 minutes (do not skimp on the time). Add the condensed milk and continue to beat until thick, 3 or 4 minutes longer. Lower the mixer speed and slowly add the key lime juice, mixing just until incorporated. Pour the mixture into the crust. Bake for 10 minutes or until the filling does not jiggle. Cool on a wire rack and then place into freezer. Freeze for 15 to 20 minutes before serving.

Before serving: whip the cream, vanilla paste, and the confectioners' sugar until stiff peaks form. Cover the pie with whipped cream and freeze an additional 20 minutes before serving. Garnish with lime zest.

Chocolate Cream Pie

This is the elusive "chocolate cream pie" that has been passed down through my family for generations. Once my grandmother died, many feared the recipe did as well. But with my mother's detective work and keen cooking skills, she was able to recreate the recipe and write it down for my sisters and me. The moral to this and all other great recipes: get it down on paper and share it with those you love!

4 T. cornstarch (6)

1 1/2 c. sugar (2 1/4)

6 T. unsweetened cocoa powder (9)

2 1/4 c. whole milk (3 3/8)

1/4 tsp. salt (1/2)

2 egg yolks (4)

3 T. unsalted butter (4 1/2)

1 1/2 tsp. vanilla (2 1/4)

1 precooked 9" piecrust

Whipped cream

Bittersweet chocolate bar

Mix cornstarch, sugar, cocoa powder, salt, and milk in a small bowl. Pour into double boiler and whisk in milk and egg yolks. Heat water in double boiler and allow chocolate mixture to cook till thick, stirring constantly with a wooden spoon. Once custard is thickened, remove from heat, stir in vanilla and butter. Stir till melted. Pour custard into prepared piecrust, and cover with plastic so it touches the custard. This will help keep a skin from forming. Allow to chill overnight. When ready to serve, top with homemade whipped cream and bittersweet chocolate shavings.

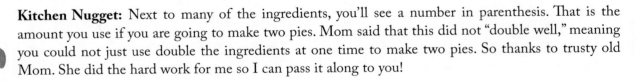

Kitchen Nugget: Next to many of the ingredients, you'll see a number in parenthesis. That is the amount you use if you are going to make two pies. Mom said that this did not "double well," meaning you could not just use double the ingredients at one time to make two pies. So thanks to trusty old Mom. She did the hard work for me so I can pass it along to you!

Guilt-free Chocolate Soufflé

Many years ago we had a steakhouse nearby that made chocolate soufflés. I fell in love! Only problem was that the word *soufflé* scared me to death. Not anymore. This is an easy recipe that anyone can make! Either make in a large round soufflé pan or in individual cups.

1 tsp. unsalted butter
1/2 c. + 1 T. sugar
6 eggs
1 tub (8 oz.) light cream cheese spread
1 T. Kahlua flavored liqueur
3 oz. bittersweet chocolate, melted (I use Ghiradelli)
1 tsp. vanilla paste

Raspberry Sauce

1 (18 oz.) jar seedless red raspberry jam
1/4 c. raspberry liqueur

Preheat oven to 350 degrees. Grease the entire inside of the soufflé pan or individual cups with butter, making sure to cover everywhere. Take 1 tablespoon of sugar and sprinkle inside ramekins, tilting pan to allow sugar to attach to butter. This will allow the soufflé not to stick after baking.

Using a hand mixer or even a blender, combine eggs, cream cheese spread, Kahlua, melted chocolate, and vanilla paste. Mix or blend till well combined and cream cheese is fully incorporated.

Pour into soufflé pan or in individual cups evenly. Place into oven and bake for 40 to 45 minutes or until puffy. While soufflés are baking, make the quick and easy raspberry sauce. In a small saucepan, warm seedless jam till liquefied. Add in liquor, and allow to cook on low heat till it reduces slightly.

Remove from stovetop and allow to cool. Remove from oven and serve immediately. Top with raspberry sauce and fresh berries.

Death by Chocolate Cake

All I can say is, "Hold on to your hat!" This is a seriously delicious chocolate cake. I make this all the time, not just because it is so moist and just the thing for a chocolate fix, but because it is so simple! Perfect for any occasion.

1 box devil's food chocolate cake mix (no pudding added)

1 small box instant chocolate fudge pudding

3 eggs, room temperature

1/2 c. warm water

1/2 c. vegetable oil

3/4 c. sour cream

1 T. flour

1 pkg. semisweet chocolate chunks

1 container chocolate fudge frosting (not whipped)

1 c. mini chocolate chips.

Preheat oven to 350 degrees. Spray a Bundt pan with nonstick cooking spray. In a large bowl, combine cake mix and fudge pudding mix. Using a hand mixer, mix in the eggs one at a time, beating slowly. Pour in water, oil, and add in sour cream. Mix together till well combined (about 2 minutes), making sure to scrape down the sides.

Using a small bowl, combine the chocolate chunks and flour together. Toss, allowing flour to coat the surface of the chunks. Add chocolate chunks to batter and just mix to combine.

Pour batter into prepared Bundt pan. Bake for 50-60 minutes or until toothpick comes out clean. Once cake is done, remove from oven. Using a piece of parchment paper laid out on your counter, invert cake onto paper, and leave the Bundt pan covering. This builds a steam "den" and makes for a super moist cake. Keep Bundt pan over cake until completely cool (about 3 hours).

Once cool, remove cake from paper and place on a plate. To make frosting, simply microwave your fudge frosting in the microwave till thick and pourable (about 30 seconds). Pour over cake and top with mini chocolate chips. Keep cake covered till ready to serve!

Mommy's Hot Fudge Sundae Cake

Each year this is my birthday cake. Now that my mom is gone, I make it, and every time I bite into the warm, moist, gooey chocolate cake, I think of Mom. This is maybe the simplest cake on the planet to make. Make it all in one 9-x-13-inch pan, and serve immediately with French vanilla ice cream. I guarantee this will be a favorite in your home.

2 c. all purpose flour
1 1/2 c. sugar
4 T. cocoa powder
4 tsp. baking powder
1/2 tsp. salt
1 c. whole milk
4 T. vegetable oil
2 tsp. vanilla
2 c. chopped pecans (optional)
2 c. brown sugar
1/2 c. cocoa powder
3 1/2 c. hottest tap water

Preheat oven to 350 degrees. In an ungreased square 9-x-13-inch casserole pan, stir together flour, sugar, 4 tablespoons cocoa, baking powder, and salt. Mix in milk, oil, and vanilla until smooth. Stir in nuts. Spread evenly in pan. Sprinkle with brown sugar and 1/2 cup cocoa. Pour hot water over batter. Bake 40 minutes. Let stand 15 minutes. Spoon into bowls, and top with French vanilla ice cream.

Variations on the tried-and-true recipe:
Hot Fudge Marshmallow Sundae Cake: add 2 cups miniature marshmallows.

Hot Fudge Coconut Sundae Cake: omit nuts; add 1 cup coconut and 1 cup chopped almonds.

Hot Fudge Butterscotch Sundae Cake: add 1 cup butterscotch pieces. Decrease brown sugar to 1 cup and the 1/2 cup cocoa to 4 tablespoons.

Hot Fudge Peanut Butter Sundae Cake: omit nuts; stir in 1 cup peanut butter (smooth or chunky) and 1/2 cup chopped peanuts.

Four-Layer Carrot Cake with Cream Cheese Frosting

This is the cake my sweet son asks for each year on his birthday. He loves it because of how high the cake sits and for the rich cream cheese frosting. I love making this for him, and thank goodness it is so darn easy. Do not be alarmed when you see baby food as an ingredient. Basically, the baby food helps skip a step and ensures you have a moist cake. Just consider this your secret. I will never tell on you!

2 c. sugar

1 1/2 c. vegetable or canola oil

4 eggs

2 tsp. vanilla or vanilla paste

3 (4 oz.) jars carrot baby food

2 c. all-purpose flour

2 tsp. baking soda

3 tsp. ground cinnamon

1 1/2 tsp. salt

1/2 c. grated carrot

1 c. flaked coconut

1 c. chopped pecans

1 (8 oz.) cream cheese, room temperature

1/4 c. unsalted butter, softened

1 tsp. vanilla paste

3-4 c. powdered sugar

Preheat oven to 350 degrees. Grease and flour 2 8-inch round cake pans. In a large bowl, beat together the sugar and vegetable oil till creamed. Add eggs and blend till well combined. Once egg, oil, and sugar are creamed together, add in baby food and vanilla.

Sift together flour, baking soda, cinnamon, and salt. Slowly add flour to the creamy mixture and beat till smooth. Add in carrots, coconut, and pecans.

Pour cake mixture into your baking pans and bake for 45-50 minutes. Allow to completely cool, and then turn out onto waxed paper. Cut cakes in 1/2, which will create 4 layers. Place first layer on plate, top with cream cheese frosting, continue on all layers, and finish by frosting top and sides. To really make this cake look fantastic, add an additional 2 cups of finely chopped pecans to the sides. Refrigerate till ready to serve.

To make frosting: With a hand mixer or a food processor, mix together the cream cheese and butter till smooth. Add in vanilla. Slowly add in powdered sugar and blend till smooth. Add more powdered sugar if necessary to reach desired thickness. Frost cake.

Kitchen Nugget: To really kick up your flavor, use Nielsen-Massey vanilla paste. Find it in your favorite gourmet store.

Chocolate Cake Dots

These little nuggets of flavor are so elegant yet so easy to make. I promise once you make them they will become a staple at all of your parties.

1 Chocolate Fudge cake mix
1 container dark chocolate frosting, not whipped style
2 (12 oz.) Wilton Candy Melts, dark cocoa
1 T. shortening

Bake cake according to package directions in a 9-x-13-inch pan. Remove the cake from the oven and allow to cool 5 minutes. In a large bowl, place cake and crumble while it is still warm. Now comes the tricky part. Start by adding 1/3 of the container of frosting; stirring to combine with the cake. Add more frosting only until the cake mixture is the consistency of stuffing. Not too loose or it will not form a firm ball. Once the mixture is firm yet holding together use a 1.25 diameter cookie scoop to make the balls. Place on a parchment–lined baking sheet. Continuing making till all of the cake is gone. Place cookie sheet in the freezer and freeze overnight.

To make chocolate topping:
Place chocolate candy melts in a bowl and melt in the microwave according to package instructions. Once chocolate is smooth, add in shortening stirring till well combined. Dip each cake ball in the chocolate and remove immediately. Place on parchment paper. To add toppings, place on top while chocolate is still soft. To add decorative lines in a complementary color simply allow coating to harden. Then melt color of your choice and pour into a plastic sandwich bag. Snip the end and squiggle over the top of your cake dots. Allow chocolate to harden and then package in decorative boxes.

Kitchen Nuggets: To make different flavors experiment with cake flavors, as well as complementary frostings. Here are a few of my favorites!

*Rainbow Chip cake mix + vanilla frosting + white chocolate melts

*Lemon cake mix + lemon frosting + white chocolate melts

*Strawberry cake mix + cream cheese frosting + white chocolate melts

*Red velvet cake mix + cream cheese frosting + white chocolate melts

*German chocolate cake mix + coconut pecan frosting + white chocolate melts

*Carrot cake + cream cheese frosting + white chocolate melts

Toppings:

*Use decorative colored candy melts

*Chopped pecans

*Mini chocolate chips

*Coconut

*Candy sprinkles

*Crushed cookies

Index

Cranberry

Cranberry Spinach Salad with Toasty Brie Bites, 44
Pan Roasted Brussels Sprouts, 80
Shaw Cranberry Slaw, 75
Slow Cooker Pork Roast with Cranberries, 88

Cream Cheese

Bigger Than Your Butt Dip, 36
Buffalo Chicken Spread, 34
Four Layer Carrot Cake with Cream Cheese Frosting, 108
Garlic Beer Cheese Soup, 32
Guilt-free Chocolate Souffle, 105
Herb Cheese Spread, 35
Mile High Peanut Butter Pie, 102
Peaches and Cream Coffee Cake, 56
Piggy Puffs, 37
Tearoom Blueberry Salad, 47

Egg

Southwest Egg Bake, 62

Grapes

Curry Chicken Salad, 43

Green Beans

Chilled Bean Salad, 76
Green Beans for the Soul, 74

Muffin

Donut Muffins, 59

Mushrooms

Steakhouse Chopped Salad, 45

Parmesan Cheese

Chipotle Grilled Asparagus, 73
Chicken Bruschetta with Balsamic Glaze, 87
Easy Weeknight Spinach Alfredo, 69
Fire Roasted Tomato Basil Soup, 51
Green Rice Casserole, 64
Piggy Puffs, 37
Potluck Macaroni Salad, 66
Southern Creamed Corn, 72

Rice

Curried Shrimp and Rice Salad, 70
Green Rice Casserole, 64

Salads

Bibb Salad with Zippy Ranch, 42
Caprese Picnic Salad with Easy Balsamic Vinaigrette, 43
Cranberry Spinach Salad with Toasty Brie Bites, 44
Potluck Macaroni Salad, 66
Steakhouse Chopped Salad, 45
Tearoom Blueberry Salad, 47

Sausage

Southwest Egg Bake, 61

Shrimp

Curried Shrimp and Rice Salad, 70
Mango Shrimp Salad Cups, 38

Spinach

Cranberry Spinach Salad with Toasty Brie Bites, 44
Steakhouse Chopped Salad, 45

Squash

Chocolate Zucchini Bread, 58
Summer Squash Casserole, 79

Tomato

Bibb Salad with Zippy Ranch, 42
Caprese Picnic Salad with Easy Balsamic Vinaigrette, 43
Chicken Bruschetta with Balsamic Glaze, 87
Family Night Goulash, 84
Fire-Roasted Tomato Basil Soup, 51
Steakhouse Chopped Salad, 45